7⁵⁴

The WANDERING JEWS

Rebellion

The Tale of the 1002nd Night

Right and Left and The Legend of the Holy Drinker

Job: The Story of a Simple Man

The Emperor's Tomb

Confession of a Murderer

The Radetzky March

Flight Without End

The Silent Prophet

Hotel Savoy

Tarabas

Weights and Measures

Zipper and His Father

The Spider's Web

The
WANDERING
JEWS

∾

Joseph Roth

TRANSLATED BY
Michael Hofmann

W. W. NORTON & COMPANY
New York • *London*

For information about permission to reproduce selections from this
book, write to Permissions, W. W. Norton & Company, Inc.,
500 Fifth Avenue, New York, NY 10110

The text of this book is composed in Bembo
with the display set in Centaur
Composition by A. W. Bennett, Inc.
Manufacturing by the Maple-Vail Book Manufacturing Group
Book design by Judith Stagnitto Abbate / ABBATE DESIGN

Library of Congress Cataloging-in-Publication Data

Roth, Joseph, 1894–1939.
[Juden auf Wanderschaft. English]
The wandering Jews / Joseph Roth ; translated by Michael Hofmann.
p. cm.
ISBN 0-393-04901-9
1. Jews—Europe, Eastern—History—20th century. 2. Jews—Identity.
3. Jews, East European—Austria—Vienna—History--20th century.
4. Jews, East European—Germany—Berlin—History—20th Century.
5. Jews, East European—France—Paris—History—20th century.
I. Title.

DS135.E8313 R67 2000

305.892'4047—dc21   00-041884

W. W. Norton & Company, Inc.,
500 Fifth Avenue, New York, N.Y. 10110
www.wwnorton.com

W. W. Norton & Company Ltd.,
10 Coptic Street, London WC1A 1PU

2 3 4 5 6 7 8 9 0

Contents

List of Illustrations

A COMMENT BY ELIE WIESEL

he *Wandering Jews* is a masterful work by Joseph Roth, a truly extraordinary writer. To read this work is to become its messenger. In these disturbing yet strikingly illuminating pages, the truth of a Jewish destiny from long ago vibrates and sings as though awakening the memory of enlightened wanderers. Everything is here: the love of an engulfed Jewish world, beautiful and moving; the passion for the wisdom of its inhabitants; the quest of the sacred by its brothers and sisters seeking a bright spot, a little peace, and, above all, the burning words that endure while all else has vanished into the madness and despair of mankind.

he *Wandering Jews* shows a side of Joseph Roth that has not yet been seen in English: the essayist, the analyst of contemporary life, the marshaler of arguments (and to a lesser degree, of facts and figures), the rhetorician, the passionate, orderly, and mobile "argufier." Admirers of Roth's fiction may be surprised at the brilliance and forcefulness of the intellect at work here—I know I was. The distinguished German critic Walter Jens described *The Wandering Jews* as the best book on its subject in German. I am astonished that, in three-quarters of a century, there seems, until now, to have been no English translation of it.

This short book emerges quite straightforwardly from Roth's professional interests and preoccupations and a little more clandestinely from his personal background and experience. The interests first: In the early 1920s, as a young journalist in Vienna and then in Berlin, Roth wrote numerous articles drawing attention to the awful plight of refugees and displaced persons—Jews and others—in the aftermath of World War One, the Russian Revolution, and the redrawing of national frontiers following the Treaty of Versailles (1919). Hundreds of thousands of people—those lucky ones who hadn't been butchered already—found themselves unhoused and persecuted, with no option but to take to the road. They sought shelter in cities and towns where most of them had never been and, unfortunately, where they were made despicably unwelcome. Roth spent a great deal of time visiting their refuges and encampments and ghettoes; he also visited their homelands. In the last five months of 1926, he toured the Soviet Union, where he wrote the final section, "The Condition of the Jews in Soviet Russia." *The Wandering Jews* was a timely and important book, one that Roth was supremely well qualified to write. That he was aware of this himself is shown by occasional outbreaks of anxiety and statistics (both very unusual in this writer). *The Wandering Jews* counters the campaigns of fear and disinformation that were mounted by the authorities and media. It shows Roth's lifelong sympathies with "simple people," the dispossessed "guests on this earth" (subtitles of two of his novels), and his antipathy to a selfish, materialistic, and increasingly homogeneous bourgeoisie. It is no accident, I think, that *The Wandering Jews* begins with a proud and rancorous castigation of that West, which Roth wants no part of: a reverse dedication.

Historically, the survival of the Jews in Europe to that

point was largely a matter of happenstance, or, at the most, of enlightened self-interest on the part of whatever country was next prepared to take them in. As one door closed, another—haltingly, opportunely, perhaps—opened. The slightest delay of course spelled instant crisis and tragedy. Roth sensed that the Twenties were such a time of crisis, and that the countries of Europe and beyond ("the land of unlimited opportunity by which of course I mean not America but Germany"), stumbling out of one war and into another, floored by inflation, willing victims of atrocious right-wing propaganda and nationalist rhetoric, would not be hospitable to the Jews who were being turned out of the East. Roth's anger in the opening pages of this book suggests that he already sensed there was little to be hoped for from—or, ten years later, *for*—the assimilated Jews in Germany, and that the Jews, always living more securely in time than space, would soon be banished to it altogether.

The Wandering Jews does two things: It describes, as Roth says, the human beings who constitute the Jewish "problem," and it casts about for a solution to that problem. In the first, it succeeds magnificently. Roth organizes his proteanly diverse subjects, and extends, it seems almost to every one of them, a unique sympathy and warmth. (The only exception being the middle-class, assimilated, denying Jews in the West.) The book is crammed with adoring portraits and analyses—it *is* an adoring analysis—of individuals and groups that are not merely heterogeneous but almost incompatible. The Jews, it seems to me, are to Roth human beings in their least packaged form. Fissured by history and geography, religiosity and class, ideology and national affiliation, mutual prejudice and the degree of their integration in their respective countries, they are the most anomalous, individual of peoples. And the more improbable, the more Roth loves them: the burly dockworker in Odessa, the elegant Parisiennes, the musical clown from Radziwillow, the young builders of Palestine, the wonder-rabbi's "front of house" man, so bewilderingly up on world affairs, and given such a glowing Noldean portrait.

So far as offering "solutions" to the "problem," that is a different matter. For all the admiration and sympathy advanced to all the various individuals and groups, it's not easy to think of one that is endorsed as the way forward: not Zionism, not ever-Westward migration, not the social experiment of the Soviet Union, and, least of all, not the abandonment of Jewishness. And yet, as Roth must have realized, the Jewish shtetl can hardly still have existed in 1926. The optimistic section on Paris frays into smaller notes on other places and ends with the desperate jab at "humanism." Even the wonderfully droll, actually rather Kafkaesque chapter on America ends with the Jew *still* excluded, *still* staring at Liberty through prison bars. It seems then that Roth moves Zeno-ishly between a past that is already over and a future that never eventuates. What is left for Roth—and this is not a solution at all—

is the destiny of the wanderer ("no home anywhere, but their graves may be found in every cemetery"). In short *The Wandering Jews* describes a problem that is not really a problem at all—more a blessing—and to which there is no solution. As one reads the 1937 Preface, one senses that all Roth is able to hope for—and this is simultaneously a cause of his greatest despair—is conditions for Jews getting steadily and bearably worse. What happened instead was the Holocaust.

I used the word "clandestinely" a while ago, and some readers may wonder: Where in all this is Joseph Roth? The answer is everywhere and nowhere, chiefly nowhere. We see him and feel him as an investigator, a "roving reporter," a trustworthy and opinionated guide—but the book rigorously excludes anything avowedly personal. We don't know that the little cruciform town in the swampy plains (described here for the first time, though it will appear later in *Job*, *Weights and Measures*, *The Leviathan*, and elsewhere) is Roth's birthplace, the town of Brody in Galicia; that the Westward momentum of the book (and again, of much of Roth's fiction) was also that of his life; that he had himself been through Vienna and Berlin, and at the time of writing, was in Paris (where he felt happiest); that his father-in-law was an installment seller in Vienna, his uncle a tailor, and his grandfather a rabbi. Finally, *nowhere does he even say he is a Jew!* I don't know why. Perhaps it was due to apprehension, or to leave himself the greatest possible freedom as he discussed the great variety of Jews, or simply because he was too proud to put his own *vita*, like a feather, on the scales. The temper of the times was not as mindlessly autobiographical as ours. Also, Roth, who loved mystification, had many different versions of himself to keep in the air. Whatever it is, the effect of so much passion and sympathy and insight being channeled through the third person is extremely odd. But it might help explain why the book seems to alternate between running freely and at times almost feeling blocked by so many things to say. There is something grimly appropriate that a book about the Jews in Europe should not accommodate its author.

Roth's friend Bruno Frei, reviewing *Flight Without End*, contended that Roth had one flaw: He only saw, he was unable to believe. That would have been in 1927. In the last twelve years of his life, it seems to me that Roth was twice able to invest things with belief. One was Judaism, in the sense of a somewhat separate presence of Jews within and throughout and inspiriting Europe; the other, the Dual Monarchy of Austria-Hungary. Both were instances of something supranational, something that contained multitudes, something not exclusive and not ideal, and therefore free from bigotry and better and broader than the run of human institutions; something whose time was—or was almost—gone. With and from these, Roth made the tragically beautiful emblematic images of his great books. I would like to give two of these.

The first is not in a book, but is a story that David

Bronsen, Roth's biographer, informs us Roth liked to tell. An old caftaned Jewish refugee, sitting in a train compartment, shows his ticket to the inspector. The inspector, suspicious, thinking that perhaps he is hiding a child in his caftan to save the price of a ticket, asks the Jew what he has in there. The Jew produces a framed portrait of Emperor Franz Joseph. The second is a little scene from *Job*, the 1930 novel in which Roth takes on the subject matter he first explores in *The Wandering Jews*: "Mendel Singer was silent. He sat by the roadside, next to Sameshkin. For the first time in his life, Mendel Singer sat on the naked earth, in the middle of the wild night, beside a peasant. [. . .] Suddenly Mendel began to sob. Mendel wept, in the midst of the strange night, next to Sameshkin. The peasant pressed his fists in his eyes, because he felt that he too would weep. Then he laid his arm around the thin shoulder of the Jew and said softly: "Sleep, dear Jew! Have a good sleep!"

—MICHAEL HOFMANN
March 2000

The WANDERING JEWS

FOREWORD

This book is not interested in the plaudits and endorsements, much less the cavils or criticisms of those who despise, hate, and persecute the Eastern European Jews. It does not address itself to those Western Europeans who, by virtue of the fact that they grew up with elevators and flush toilets, allow themselves to make bad jokes about Romanian lice, Galician cockroaches, or Russian fleas. This book is not interested in those "objective" readers who peer down with a cheap and sour benevolence from the rickety towers of their Western civilization upon the near East and its inhabitants; who, out of sheer humanity, are struck with pity at inadequate sewage systems, and whose fear of contagion leads them to lock up poor immigrants in tenements where social problems are solved by simple epidemics. This book does not want to be read by those who would seek to deny their own fathers or forefathers if they happened to escape from such tenements. This book has not been written for readers who would blame the author for treating the subjects of his account with love, and not with that "scientific detachment" better known as indifference.

So, for whom is this book?

The author has the fond hope that there may still be readers from whom the Eastern Jews do not require protection: readers with respect for pain, for human greatness, and for the squalor that everywhere accompanies misery; Western Europeans who are not merely proud of their clean mattresses. These are readers who feel they might have something to learn from the East, and who have perhaps already sensed that great people and great ideas—great but also useful (to them)—have come from Galicia, Russia, Lithuania, and Romania; ideas that would help shore up and expand the firm foundations of Western civilization. These are readers who have already perceived that these "visitors from the East"—as the local news report, the meanest product of Western Europe, likes to call them—are not just pickpockets.

This book will unfortunately not be able to treat the problem of Eastern Jewry with the comprehensiveness and thoroughness that it needs and deserves. It will only try to describe the human beings who constitute the problem, and the circumstances that cause it. It will report only on parts of a huge mass of material that, to be dealt with in its entirety, would demand of the author personally as many wanderings as have been suffered by several entire generations of Eastern Jews.

EASTERN EUROPEAN JEWS IN THE WEST

he Eastern Jew in his homeland knows nothing of the social injustice of the West; nothing of the habitual bias that governs the actions, decisions, and opinions of the average Western European; nothing of the narrowness of the Western perspective, jagged with factory smokestacks and framed by power plants; nothing of the sheer hatred that, like a life-prolonging (though lethal) drug, is so powerful that it is tended like a sort of Eternal Flame, at which these selfish people and nations warm themselves. The Eastern Jew looks to the West with a longing that it really doesn't merit. To the Eastern Jew, the West signifies freedom, justice, civilization, and the possibility to work and develop his talents. The West exports engineers, automobiles, books, and poems to the East. It sends propaganda soaps and hygiene, useful and elevating things, all of them beguiling and come-hitherish to the East. To the Eastern Jew, Germany, for example, remains the land of Goethe and

Schiller, of the German poets, with whom every keen Jewish youth is far more conversant than our own swastika'd secondary school pupils. In the course of the War the Eastern Jew was lucky enough to come across the general who issued a high-sounding proclamation to the Polish Yids— drafted for him by his press department—not that other general who never read a single work of literature but managed to lose the war, just the same.

And so, conversely, the Eastern Jew sees none of the advantages of his own homeland. He sees nothing of the boundless horizon, nothing of the quality of the people, in whom simplicity can produce holy men and murderers, melodies of melancholy, grandeur, and obsessive passion. He fails to see the goodness of the Slav people, whose coarseness remains more decent than the housetrained animality of the Western European, his secretive perversions, his cringing before the law, with his wellbred hat in his apprehensive hand.

The Eastern Jew fails to see the beauty of the East. He has not been allowed to live in villages or in big cities. Here Jews live in dirty streets and collapsing houses. Their Christian neighbor threatens them. The local squire beats them. The official has them locked up. The army officer fires his gun at them with impunity. The dog barks at them, because their garb seems to provoke animals and primitive people alike. They are brought up in dark *heders*. The painful perspectivelessness of the Jewish prayer is something they are made acquainted with in early childhood; the passionate wrangling with a God who is more a vengeful God than a loving God, who condemns pleasure as much as sin; the strict compulsion to study and pursue abstractions with young eyes that have never really seen.

For the most part, Eastern Jews experience the countryside only as beggars or vagrants. The majority don't understand the soil that feeds them. The Eastern Jew feels apprehensive in unfamiliar villages and forests. He is a case apart, partly from choice, partly by force. He has obligations and no rights, except on paper, where they count for nothing. Newspapers, books, and optimistic emigrants all tell him what a paradise the West is. In Western Europe there is legal protection from pogroms. In Western Europe Jews may become government ministers or even viceroys. Many Eastern European dwellings have pictures of Moses Montefiore, who dined regularly at the table of the king of England. The great wealth of the Rothschilds is exaggerated to fairy-tale proportions in the East. From time to time an emigrant will send word home, pointing out all the advantages of the new life abroad. Most Jewish emigrants are too proud to write when things are going badly for them, and most are eager to play up the new home at the expense of the old. They have the naive desire of the small-town boy to cut a dash in front of his erstwhile fellows. In a small town in the East, a letter from an émigré creates a huge stir. All the young people in the place—and not a few of the old—are overcome by itchy feet. They want to leave the country where a war might break out from one year to the next, and from one week to the next, a pogrom. And so they leave, on foot, by train, on board ship, for Western countries where a different, somewhat reformed though no less dismal, ghetto offers its own brand of darkness to the newcomers who have barely managed to escape the clutches of the concentration camp.

When I referred just now to Jews who are completely alienated from the earth that nourishes them, I was referring to the majority of Jews: those who live by the old laws and customs of their Jewish faith. Of course there are also Jews who fear neither the dog nor his master, neither the policeman nor the army officer, who don't live in a ghetto, who have adopted the culture and the language of their host-nation. They are similar to Western Jews, but are actually more likely than Western Jews to enjoy social equality; and yet they are still kept from freely developing their talents unless they convert from Judaism, and even then things are far from easy. Because each fortunate assimilant will inevitably keep a thoroughly Jewish set of relatives, and it would be a rare judge or attorney or general practitioner of Jewish extraction who didn't have, say, a cousin, uncle, or grandfather whose mere physical appearance might not put an end to a promising career or at least do him social damage.

It is hard to avoid such a fate. And so, instead of running away from it, many decide to do the opposite. They

throw themselves into fate's arms, not only by not denying their Jewishness but by emphasizing it at every turn
and proclaiming their allegiance to a "Jewish nation"
whose existence has for several decades now been indis-
putable, and whose "right to exist" is similarly unarguable.
The will of several million people is already enough to
form a "nation," even if it has not existed before.

The idea of a Jewish nationalism is very much alive in
the East. Even people who themselves have little truck
with the language, culture, and religion of their forefathers
claim membership of the "Jewish nation" on the basis
of their will and their race. They constitute a "national
minority" in a foreign country, striving for their rights as
citizens and nationals. Some look toward a future in Palestine, and some, rightly believing that the earth belongs to
everyone who treats it with respect, have no national aspirations. (But in either case they are unable to extinguish
the primitive hatred that burns so corrosively in their
host-people for what seem to them a dangerous number
of foreigners.) These Jews no longer live in the ghetto
either, nor even in their warm and true traditions. They
are deracinated as their assimilated brothers are, sometimes
to the point of heroism, because they are the willing victims of an idea—even if it's nothing better than the idea
of a nation. . . .

Both the nationalists and the assimilated Jews tend to
remain in the East. The former because they want to fight
for rights where they are, the latter because they imagine

they are already in possession of such rights, or because they love the country as much as the Christian population does. The ones who emigrate are those who have wearied of the petty but unremitting struggle, and who either know or feel or merely guess that a different set of problems presents itself in the West; that the national squabbles there are just a hollow echo of yesterday's; that the West has a vision of Europe, which, maybe one day, not before time and not without suffering, will ripen into a vision of the world. These Jews prefer to live in countries where questions of race and nationality may still excite the interest of large and even powerful sections of the population, but these sections are already a little behind the times. There is a faint but unignorable whiff of mold, blood, and low intelligence about them, and for all their efforts, a few, more progressive minds are already grappling with the problems of tomorrow. (These emigrants, be it noted, come from the Russian borderlands, not from Russia itself.) Others may emigrate because they have lost—or have never been able to find—work and a means of support. They are seekers after bread, proletarians, albeit not always with a proletarian consciousness. Others have fled the War and the Revolution. They are "refugees," generally middle class or lower middle, implacable enemies of the Revolution, and more deeply conservative than any landowning aristocrat could ever be.

Many are wanderers by instinct, not really knowing why. They follow a vague call from elsewhere or a specific one from some relocated relative, the desire to see something of the world and escape the supposed constraints of home, the will to work and make something of themselves.

Many return. Many more remain by the wayside. Eastern Jews have no home anywhere, but their graves may be found in every cemetery. Many grow rich. Many achieve fame. Many make outstanding contributions to foreign cultures. Many lose both themselves and the world. Many remain in the ghetto, and it is only their children who will leave it. Most give the West at least as much as it takes from them. Some give it more than it gives them. The right to live in the West belongs to anyone who sacrifices himself by going to look for it.

Anyone deserves the West who arrives with fresh energy to break up the deadly, antiseptic boredom of its civilization, prepared to undergo the quarantine that we prescribe for immigrants. We do not realize that our whole life has become a quarantine, and that all our countries have become barracks and concentration camps, admittedly with all the modern conveniences. The immigrants—alas!—do not assimilate too slowly, as they are accused of doing, but if anything much too quickly to our sorry way of living. Yes, they go on to become diplomats and journalists, mayors and dignitaries, police inspectors and bank managers, as much pillars of the community as any of the natives. Only a very few are revolutionaries. Many are socialists from personal necessity. In the type of society that socialism would bring about, the oppression of a race is impossible. Many see anti-Semitism as an expression of the capitalist economy, though that isn't what makes them socialists. They are socialists because they are oppressed.

The majority are working class or lower-middle class, without proletarian consciousness. Many are instinctively reactionary, from love of property and tradition, but also from the not unjustified apprehension that change would not necessarily improve things for the Jews. There is a historical feeling, based on plentiful experience, that the Jews will be the first victims in the event of a bloodbath.

Perhaps that's what makes the Jewish worker so patient and calm. The Jewish intellectual may give the revolutionary movement inspiration and focus with his passionate engagement. The Eastern Jewish laborer, in his love of work, his sober cast of thought, his quiet life, is comparable to the German.

Because they do exist, Eastern Jewish workers—I assume that this still needs saying, in a country where the public prints like to harp on about "the unproductive mass of Eastern immigrants." There are Eastern Jewish workers, Jews who don't know how to dicker, trade, undercut, or "calculate," who don't deal in secondhand clothing, don't go from house to house with their bundles, though they are often forced to take up such sad and humiliating trades because no factory will take them, because here in Western Europe there are laws (ones I'm sure are necessary) to protect native-born workers from the competition of aliens. Even if such laws didn't exist, the prejudices of employers and also of their trade union brethren would make the Jewish worker an impossibility. In the United States he is by no means uncommon. But in Western Europe he is unheard of and his very existence denied.

Similarly denied in the West is the Jewish craftsman. The East has its share of Jewish plumbers, carpenters, cobblers, tailors, furriers, coopers, glaziers, and roofers. The notion of an Eastern Europe in which all the Jews are either wonder-rabbis or traders, and the entire Christian population is made up of peasants who live under one roof with their pigs, and noblemen who do nothing but hunt and drink, is just as ridiculous as the Eastern Jew's dream of the humanistic West. In the East thinkers and poets* are actually more commonly met with than wonder-rabbis and traders. Apart from which, it is perfectly possible for wonder-rabbis and even traders to moonlight as thinkers and poets, which is something that seems rather beyond, say, a Western European general.

The War, the Revolution in Russia, and the collapse of the Austro-Hungarian monarchy have all increased the number of Jewish immigrants to the West, who certainly haven't come to spread the plague, the terrors of war, or

---

*Dichter und Denker. The land of thinkers and poets is, of course, Germany. Sometimes this has been changed to Richter und Henker, judges and hangmen.

the (somewhat exaggerated) horrors of the Revolution.
They are even less impressed with the hospitality of the
West than is the West with the arrival of these unbidden
guests. (Eastern Jews received Western troops in quite a
different spirit.) Finding themselves, like it or not, in the
West, they had to find a way of getting by there. And they
found it most readily in trade, which is not an easy profession. They gave themselves up and became traders in
the West.

They gave themselves up. They lost themselves. They
shed their aura of sad beauty. Instead a dust-gray layer of
suffering without meaning and anxiety without tragedy
settled on their stooped backs. Contempt clung to them—
when previously only stones had been able to reach them.
They made compromises. They changed their garb, their
beards, their hair, their mode of worship, their Sabbath,
their household—they themselves might still observe the
traditions, but the traditions loosened themselves a little
from them. They became ordinary little middle-class people. The worries of the middle classes became their worries. They paid their taxes, they received police registration
forms, they registered, and they assigned themselves to
a "nationality," to a "citizenship," which, after many
chicanes, was finally "granted" to them. They used the
streetcars, the elevators, all the benedictions of modern
civilization. They even had a "fatherland."

It is a provisional fatherland. National aspirations are
alive in the Eastern Jew, even if he is half-assimilated to

the ways and habits of the West. Zionism and nationhood are by their nature Western European ideals, even if what they aspire towards may not be. Only in the East do people live who are unconcerned with their "nationality," in the Western European sense. They speak several languages, are themselves the product of several generations of mixed marriages, and fatherland for them is whichever country happens to conscript them. The Armenians of the Caucasus were for a long time neither Russians nor Armenians; they were Muslims living in the Caucasus, and yet they furnished the czars of Russia with their most loyal bodyguards. Nationality is a Western concept. It was an invention of Western European scholars, who ever since have struggled to explain it. The old Dual Monarchy of Austria-Hungary gave them, apparently, their best evidence of nationalism in action. In fact, if it had been at all well governed it could just as easily have provided evidence for the opposite. The incompetence of its governments furnished the evidence for a mistaken theory, founded on mistakes and given further credence by mistakes. The cradle of modern Zionism was Austria, was Vienna. It was founded by an Austrian journalist.* No one else could have founded it. The Austrian parliament was where the representatives of the various nationalities sat, engaged in fighting for national rights and freedoms that would have been perfectly unremarkable if they had

*Theodor Herzl (1860–1904), initially an assimilationist, later a Zionist.

been conceded. The Austrian parliament was like a bat-
tlefield for the various competing nationalisms. If the
Czechs were promised a new school, the German community in Bohemia felt aggrieved. And if the Poles in
East Galicia were given a Polish-speaking governor, then
the Ruthenians felt their noses were out of joint. Every
nationality within Austria–Hungary pressed its claims on
the basis of its "territory." Only the Jews ("soil" was the
word used in their case) had no territory of their own. In
Galicia the majority of them were neither Poles nor
Ruthenian. However, anti-Semitism was to be found
equally among Germans and Czechs, Poles and Ratheni-
ans, Magyars and Romanians in Transylvania. They managed to refute the proverb that says that when two
quarrel, the third is the winner. The Jews were always the
third party, and they always lost. Then they pulled themselves together and came out in favor of a Jewish nation
of their own. They compensated for the lack of any "soil"
to call their own in Europe by aspiring to a home in
Palestine. They had always lived in exile anyway. Now
they became a nation in exile. They sent Jewish nationalist representatives to the Austrian parliament and began to
agitate for rights and freedoms as a nation before they had
been accorded even the most basic ones as humans.

"National self-determination" was the battle cry all
over Europe, and the Jews took it up as well. The Treaty
of Versailles and the League of Nations did all they could

to ensure the Jews' right to nationhood. Today the Jews constitute a "national minority" in many countries. They don't have everything they want, but they have a lot: their own schools, the right to their own language, and several other rights of the sort that are supposed to confer happiness in Europe.

But even if the Jews were to succeed in acquiring all the rights of a "national minority" in Poland, in Czechoslovakia, in Romania, in the German-speaking part of Austria, it would still beg the great question of whether the Jews are not actually a far bigger thing altogether than a European-style national minority; whether they are not indeed more than a "nation" in the European sense; and whether, in pressing their entitlement to "national rights," they are not renouncing far more important claims.

What bliss to become a "nation," no different from the Germans, the French, or the Italians, having already been a "nation" themselves for over three thousand years and fought "holy wars" and experienced periods of greatness! Having beheaded enemy generals and overcome one's own. The era of "national history" and "patriotic studies" lies way back in the Jewish past. Jews patrolled and defended their own borders; conquered cities; crowned kings; paid taxes; were subjects; had "enemies"; were taken prisoner; dabbled in global politics; brought down cabinet ministers; had a kind of university, with professors and students; a stuck-up caste of priests, wealth and poverty, prostitution, ownership and penury, masters and slaves. Do they want all that again? Can it be that they're *envious* of European states?

Certainly they want more than merely to safeguard their "national characteristics." They want their rights to life, health, and liberty, rights that in almost every European country they are denied outright or have only in curtailed form. Truly Palestine is witnessing a national rebirth. The young *halutzim* are brave farmers and workers, and they demonstrate the willingness of the Jew to work and till the fields and become sons of the soil, in spite of having spent hundreds of years among books. Unfortunately the *halutzim* are also obliged to take up arms, to be soldiers, and to protect the land against the Arabs. Thus the European example has been carried into Palestine. Unfortunately, the young *halutz* is not only a returnee to the land of his forefathers and a proletarian with the righteous outlook of a workingman; he is also the disseminator of a culture. He is as much a European as he is a Jew. He brings the Arabs electricity, fountain pens, engineers, machine guns, shallow philosophies, and all the other things that come out of England. Of course the Arabs ought to be grateful for the fine new roads. But the instincts of a people close to nature quite rightly rebel against the onslaught of an Anglo-American civilization, all in the honorable name of national rebirth. The Jew has a right to Palestine, not because he once came from there but because no other country will have him. The Arab's fear for his freedom is just as easy to understand as the Jew's genuine intention to play fair by his neighbor. And despite all that, the immigration of young Jews into Palestine increasingly suggests a kind of Jewish Crusade, because, unfortunately, they also shoot.

Even if the Jews reject Europe's bad habits and customs, they aren't quite able to do without them. They are themselves Europeans. The Jewish governor of Palestine is beyond question an Englishman. He's probably even an Englishman first and Jew second. The Jews are either victims or helpless tools of European politics. They are exploited or abused. At any rate it will be difficult for them to become a nation with a completely new, un-European physiognomy. The European mark of Cain won't wash off. It is surely better to be a nation than to be maltreated by one. But it's a painful necessity all the same. Where's the pride for the Jew, who disarmed long ago, in proving once more that he is capable of squad drill!

Because actually the world isn't made up of "nations" and fatherlands, that want only to preserve their cultural distinctions, and only if it means not sacrificing a single human life. Fatherlands and nations want much more, or much less: They have vested interests that insist on sacrifices. They set up a series of "fronts" in order to secure the "hinterland" that is their real objective. Given all the millennial grief of the Jews, they still had one consolation: the fact that they *didn't* have such a fatherland. If there can ever be such a thing as a just history, surely the Jews will be given great credit for holding on to their common sense in not having had a fatherland at a time when the whole world launched itself into patriotic madness.

They have no fatherland, the Jews, but every country in which they live and pay their taxes looks to them for patriotic commitment and heroism, and reproaches them for dying without enthusiasm. In these circumstances Zionism is really the only way out: If one must be patriotic, then at least let it be for a country of one's own.

But for as long as Jews continue to live in the countries of others, they are required to live and, unfortunately, also to die for these countries. Yes, there are even some Jews who live and die for these countries with enthusiasm. There are Eastern Jews who have assimilated to the country of their choice, and have completely adopted the local set of values, including "fatherland," "duty," "a hero's death," and "war loans." They have become Western Jews, Western Europeans.

But what makes a "Western Jew"? Is it that he can prove that his ancestors were fortunate enough never to have had to flee from any Western European, not to say German, pogroms, in the Middle Ages or subsequently? Is a Jew from the city of Breslau, long known by its Polish name of Wroclaw, more of a Western Jew than one from Cracow, which is still in Poland today? Is a man a Western Jew if his father has no memories of Posen or Lvov? Almost all Jews were Western before they ever got to

Russia or Poland. And all Jews were once "Eastern Jews," before a few of them went West. Half of all the Jews who today speak contemptuously or disparagingly of the East had grandfathers who came from Tarnopol.* And if they weren't, then it was by sheer, blind fortune. How easy in the course of a pogrom to end up suddenly in the East, where they hadn't yet begun beating their Jews!

All that makes it unfair to assert that a Jew who came to Germany from the East in 1914 had any lesser understanding of war loans or draft boards than a Jew whose ancestors had lent money or been drafted for the past three hundred years. The more imbecilic the immigrant, the sooner he bought war bonds. Many Jews, Eastern Jews, or the sons and grandsons of Eastern Jews died in the War fighting for one or other of the countries of Europe. I don't say this to exonerate the Eastern Jews. On the contrary: *I blame them for it*.

They died, suffered, caught typhoid, supplied "spiritual counselors" for the field, even though Jews are allowed to die without a rabbi and stand in even less need of some padre's patriotic rhetoric than their Christian fellows. They fell in with Western abuses and bad habits. They assimilated. They no longer pray in synagogues and prayerhouses, but in boring temples where the worship is as mechanical as it is in the better class of Protestant

*Now Ternopil.

church. They came to be temple Jews, in other words: well-bred, clean-shaven gentlemen in morning coats and top hats, who wrap their prayer book in the editorial page of the Jewish newspaper in the belief that it will attract less attention that way. Organ sounds are heard in the temple, and the cantor and rabbi wear headgear that might have been borrowed from a Christian minister. Any Protestant blundering into a Jewish temple would have to admit that the difference between Jew and Christian is not that great, and he might even give up his anti-Semitism if it wasn't that he had such keen business competition from the Jews.

Their grandfathers were still engaged in a desperate struggle with Jehovah, bruised their foreheads on the drab walls of the small prayerhouse, called out for their sins to be punished and begged for forgiveness. The grandsons have become Westerners. They need the organ to put them in the mood, their God is a redaction of nature, their prayer a formula. And on top of that they're proud of it! They're lieutenants in the reserve, and their God is a commanding officer, the same God by whose grace the kings sat on their thrones.

And the name for all this is Western civilization. Whoever has it is entitled to despise his cousin who, authentic and uncontaminated, comes from the East. Such an Eastern Jew has within himself more humanity and more divinity than all the preachers can come up with in all the theological colleges of Western Europe.

With luck the cousin will have the fortitude not to lapse into assimilation.

In what follows, I will attempt to describe how the Eastern Jew and his kind live, first at home and then abroad.

THE JEWISH SHTETL

he little town lies in the middle of a great plain, not bounded by any hill or forest or river. It runs out into the plain. It begins with little huts and ends with them. After a while the huts are replaced by houses. Streets begin. One runs from north to south, the other from east to west. Where they intersect is the marketplace. At the far end of the north-south street is the railway station. A passenger train calls in once a day. A passenger train pulls out once a day. And yet, many people spend their entire day at the station. They are traders. Their interest legitimately extends to freight trains. In addition they take urgent letters to the station, because the town's letterboxes are only emptied once a day. It is a fifteen-minute walk from the shtetl to the station. When it's raining you have to take a cab, because the street is underwater, it's so poorly made. Poor people get together to share a cab, which can accommodate six people, though not exactly seat them. The rich man sits in the cab by himself and pays more for the ride than the six poor people. There are eight cabs available for hire. Six of them are one-horse carriages. The two two-horse carriages are for important visitors, who sometimes happen into town. The eight cabbies are Jews. They are devout Jews who don't trim their beards but don't wear the long robes of their fellow believers. They are better able to pursue their profession in short jerkins. They don't drive on the Sabbath. On the Sabbath no one has any business at the station anyway. The town has eighteen thousand inhabitants, of whom fifteen thousand are Jews. Of the three thousand Christians, a hundred might be traders and merchants; another hundred, officials; one notary; one doctor; and eight policemen. There are actually ten policemen in all, but, bizarrely, two of them are Jews. What the other Christians do I'm not actually sure. Of the fifteen thousand Jews, eight thousand live from trade. They are small merchants, bigger merchants, and big merchants. The remaining seven thousand Jews are small artisans, laborers, water carriers, scholars, synagogue officials, and servants. They are teachers, scribes, Torah scribes, tallith weavers, doctors, lawyers, officials, beggars and paupers too ashamed to live on public welfare, as well as gravediggers, circumcisers, and gravestone cutters.

The town has two churches, a synagogue, and some forty little prayerhouses. The Jews go to pray three times a day. They would have to undertake the walk to the synagogue and back to their homes or shops six times a day, if they didn't have so many prayerhouses, in which, incidentally, one doesn't just pray, but also learns Jewish lore. There are Jewish scholars who, corresponding to European researchers in libraries, study in the prayerhouse from five in the morning until midnight. On the Sabbath and on holy days they go home to take their meals. Unless they happen to have patrons or private means, they live off small gifts from the community and off occasional devout works, for instance: acting as cantor, teaching, or blowing the shofar on High Holy Days. Their families, their homes, their children are all the responsibility of their wives, who carry on a small trade with maize in summer and naphtha in winter, as well as pickled cucumbers, beans, and baked goods.

The traders and other lay Jews say their prayers very quickly and leave themselves time to discuss current events and politics on the great and small stage. They smoke cigarettes and bad pipe tobacco in the prayerhouse. They treat it like an officers' mess. They are not rare visitors of God, they live with him. They don't make official state visits, they gather three times a day at his rich, poor, holy tables. In their prayers they inveigh against him, they cry to high heaven, they complain at his severity, they go to God to accuse God, and then go on to admit that they have sinned, that their punishments were just, and that they will be better in the future. There is no other people that lives on such a footing with their god. They are an old people and they have known him a long time! They have experienced

27

his great goodness and his cold justice. They have sinned often and repented bitterly, and they know that while they may be punished they will never be abandoned.

To the outsider, all prayerhouses look the same. They aren't, of course, and many of them use different forms of worship. While there are no sects as such in Judaism, there are various sectlike groupings. There is an implacably severe and a more moderate Orthodoxy. There are "Ashkenazi" and "Sephardic" prayers, and small textual variants in the same prayers.

Very clearly marked is the distinction between so-called enlightened Jews and the cabalists, the followers of various individual wonder-rabbis, each of whom has his own personal group of hasids. The enlightened Jews are not by any means unbelieving. They merely reject any form of mysticism, and their unshakable faith in the miracles related in Scripture remains completely unaffected by the unbelief with which they confront the miracles of contemporary rabbis. For the hasids, however, the wonder-rabbi is the intercessor between man and God. The enlightened Jews have no need of any such intercessor. They prefer to do their own advocacy before him, regarding it as a sin to believe in any earthly power capable of anticipating God's wisdom. And yet many Jews, even if they are not hasids, are unable to resist the wonderful atmosphere that wafts around a rabbi, and unbelieving Jews and even the occasional Christian peasant like to seek out a rabbi for help and solace when they are in difficulties.

To outsiders and enemies, Eastern Jews like to present a united front, or what appears to be a united front. Nothing gets through to the outside world of the zeal with which individual groups fight one another, the hatred and the bitterness with which the supporters of one wonder-rabbi assail those of another, or the contempt all devout Jews have for those sons of their tribe who have conformed to the customs and dress of their Christian surroundings. Most devout Jews are unsparing in their condemnation of the man who shaves his beard—the clean-shaven face serving as the visible sign of breaking with the faith. The clean-shaven Jew no longer sports the badge of his people. He attempts, perhaps unconsciously, to ape those happy Christians who are not mocked or persecuted. Though even that isn't enough for him to escape anti-Semitism. Anyway, it remains the obligation of the Jews to look to God, and not to their fellow man, for some relief of their position. Any form of assimilation, even the most superficial, constitutes flight or attempted flight from the sad society of the persecuted—an attempt to gloss over differences that aren't so easily gotten rid of.

There are no longer borders that protect against miscegenation. Therefore every Jew erects borders around himself. It would be a shame to give them up. Because however great the need, the future will bring the most magnificent deliverance. The apparent cowardice of the Jew who doesn't respond to the stone thrown at him by the child and who seems deaf to the shouted insult is, in fact, the pride of someone who knows that he will one day prevail. He knows that nothing can happen to him except by God's will, and that nothing will shield him from harm as sublimely as God's will. Has he not happily allowed himself to be burned? What can a pebble do to hurt him; how can the saliva of a rabid dog harm him? The contempt that the Eastern Jew feels for the unbeliever is a thousand times greater than any that is directed at him. What is the rich nobleman, the police officer, the general, the governor, compared to a single word of God, one of those words that a Jew always has in his heart? Even as he greets the nobleman, he laughs at him. What does the nobleman know of the inner meaning of life? Even if he had wisdom, his wisdom would be froth on the surface of things. He may know the laws of the land, build railways, invent all manner of curious things, write books, and go hunting with kings. But what are all these compared to a tiny character in the Holy Scripture, compared to the most ignorant question from the youngest Talmud student?

The Jew who thinks like this will not be greatly interested in any law that promises him personal and national liberty. Nothing truly good can come to him from people. In fact it is almost a sin to try to secure something from them. This Jew is not a "nationalist" in the Western sense. He is God's Jew. He does not fight for any Palestine. He detests the Zionist, who uses ridiculous European methods to try to set up a Judaism that doesn't deserve the name, because it won't abide the coming of the Messiah and God's change of heart, which are sure to come. In that crazy stubbornness, there is as much courage and spirit of sacrifice as there is in the bravery of the young *halutzim* who are building Palestine—even though the one may attain an end and the other its own destruction. There can be no compromise between that Orthodoxy and the kind of Zionism that will build roads even on the Sabbath. An Orthodox hasid from the East will prefer a Christian to a Zionist. For the latter would change Judaism root and branch. His Jewish nation would be along the lines of a European state. The outcome might be a sovereign nation, but it wouldn't have any Jews in it. These Jews have failed to notice that progress is destroying the Jewish religion, that fewer and fewer believers are holding out, and that the numbers of the faithful are dwindling. They fail to make any connection between developments in the wider world and developments in Judaism. They have a lofty and a mistaken way of thinking.

Many Orthodox Jews have allowed themselves to be persuaded. They no longer see in the shaved beard the mark of the defector. Their children and grandchildren go to work in Palestine. Their children become Jewish nationalist politicians. They have accepted how things are and have reconciled themselves to it, but they still have not ceased to believe in the miracle of the Messiah. They have made compromises.

Still bitter and unreconciled, however, are a great many hasids, who occupy a very remarkable position within Judaism. To the Western European they are as exotic and remote as, say, the inhabitants of the Himalayan region, who are now so much in fashion.* In fact they are even more mysterious, because, being more prudent than those other helpless objects of European inquisitiveness, they have already come to know the superficial civilization of Europe, and they are resolutely unimpressed by such things as film projectors, or binoculars or airplanes. But even if their naïveté and their hospitality had been as great as those of other people who have suffered at the hands of our desire for knowledge, even then it would be hard to persuade a European man of learning to embark on a voyage of discovery among the hasids. The Jew, because he lives everywhere in our midst, has ostensibly already been "researched." Meanwhile, the things that happen at the court of a wonder-rabbi are at least as interesting as with your Indian fakir.

There are many wonder-rabbis living in the East, and each one is reckoned by his supporters to be the greatest. The calling of wonder-rabbi has been handed down from father to son for generations. Each one holds court, and each one has his lifeguard of hasids, who come and go in his house, fast and pray, and take their meals with him. He has the power of blessing, and his blessing is efficacious. He can curse too, and his curse will blight an entire fam-

*In *Right and Left* (1930), Roth sardonically describes the East as "extending from Katowice as far as Rabindranath Tagore."

ily. Woe betide the skeptic who talks dismissively about him. Fortunate the believer who comes to him bearing gifts. The rabbi doesn't take them for himself. He lives more modestly than the meanest beggar. He eats only so much as will barely keep him alive. He lives only that he may serve God. He takes small morsels of food and small sups of drink. When he sits at a table among his people, he takes a single mouthful from the richly heaped plate in front of him, and then he sends the rest around the table. Every guest is sent away replete with the rabbi's food. He himself knows no physical needs. The enjoyment of his wife is a sacred duty to him and is a pleasure only because it is a duty. He must sire children so that the people of Israel should be as numerous as the sand on the shore or the stars in the sky. All other women are banished from his immediate circle. Food, too, is not food, so much as thanks to the Creator for the miracle of food and obedience to the injunction to nourish himself from the fruits of the earth and the flesh of beasts—which God has created for mankind. Day and night the rabbi reads in his holy books. Many of them he has read so many times that he knows them by heart. But every word, every letter even, contains millions of pages, and every page tells of the greatness of God, never sufficiently to be learned.

Day after day people come to him with a dear friend who has fallen ill or a mother who is dying, who are threatened with imprisonment or are wanted by the authorities, whose son has been called up so that he may drill on behalf of strangers and die on behalf of strangers in their senseless war. Or by those whose wives are barren and who want a son. Or by people who are faced with a great decision and are uncertain what to do. The rabbi helps and intercedes not only between man and God, but between man and his fellow man, which is still harder. People come to him from far afield. In the course of a single year, he hears the most extraordinary stories, and no case is so complicated that he hasn't already heard one that was still more so. The rabbi has wisdom and experience in equal measure; he has as much practical common sense as he has confidence in himself and his mission. He is able to offer advice or prayer. He has learned to interpret the sentences of Scripture and the instructions of God in a way that does not bring them into conflict with the laws of earthly life, and he leaves no little chinks anywhere through which a liar might manage to slip. Since the first day of Creation, many things have changed but not the will of God, which expresses itself in the basic laws of the world. There is no need of any compromises to prove that. Everything is just a question of understanding. Whoever has seen as much as the rabbi is already beyond the reach of doubt. He has left the stage of wisdom behind him. The circle is unbroken. Man is once more a believer. The arrogant science of the surgeon kills the patient, and the empty knowledge of the physicist leads his students into error. One no longer believes the knower. One believes the believer.

Many believe in him. He himself, the rabbi, does not distinguish between the most faithful followers of the Scriptures and the somewhat less faithful ones, no, nor even between Jew and *goy* or man and beast. Whoever comes to him is assured of getting his help. He knows more than he is permitted to say. He knows that there is another world above this one, which is differently constituted, and he may even sense that certain commands and interdictions that make sense in this world are of no consequence in the other. What matters to him is following these unwritten, but all the more valid, laws.

People lay siege to his house. It is larger, brighter, wider than Jewish dwellings generally are. Some wonder-rabbis really do hold court. Their wives wear exquisite dresses and have servants; they own horses and stables—not for the enjoyment of them, mind, but in order to represent.

IT WAS on a day in late autumn that I set out to call on the rabbi. A day in late autumn in the East, still warm, full of humility and a golden forbearance. I got up at five in the morning. The cold damp fogs were lifting, and visible shivers passed over the backs of the patient horses. Five Jewish women sat in the farm cart with me. They wore black woolen cloths and looked older than their years. A hard life had marked their bodies and their faces. They were traders, bringing poultry to the houses of the well-to-do and living off their slender profits. All of them had their young children with them. With whom could they have left them anyway, on a day when the whole world was off to see the rabbi?

We reached the small town where the rabbi lived just as day was breaking, and we saw that many people were there ahead of us. These people had been there sometimes for days already, sleeping in passageways, in barns, in hay-lofts. The local Jews were doing good business, renting out places to sleep for money. The large inn was overcrowded. The street was uneven, rotten fence planks stood in for pavements, and squatting on the planks were the people.

I had on a short fur coat and high riding boots. I no doubt looked like one of the feared local officials, a signal from whom was enough to get someone thrown into prison. Therefore people let me pass. They moved aside for me and were surprised that I thanked them. Outside the rabbi's house stood a red-haired Jew, the master of ceremonies, beset on all sides with pleading and cursing, with nudges and with banknotes, a man of influence who knew no mercy. He repelled the imploring and the scolding alike with a kind of measured roughness. Indeed, it sometimes happened that he took money from some people and then didn't admit them, that he forgot who had given him money or affected to have forgotten it. His face was waxy white and shaded by a round black velvet hat. His copper-colored beard jutted into people's faces in disorderly tufts, in places it had worn out like an old lin-ing, and where it did have a showing, it grew as it pleased, not subject to the design that nature has planned for the run of beards. The Jew had small yellow eyes under very thin, scarcely visible eyebrows; broad strong jaws that suggested an admixture of Slavic blood; and pale, bluish lips. When he shouted I saw his strong yellow teeth, and when he pushed someone away, I saw his powerful hand, sprinkled with red hairs.

I gave the man a signal I thought he'd understand. It meant: Here is something rather out of the ordinary, something we need to talk about in private. He vanished. He slammed the door, locked it, and, parting the crowds, came up to me.

"I'm not from here, I've come from afar, and I would like to speak to the rabbi. Only I'm not able to give you much money."

"If someone is sick, or you want a prayer said for his cure, or if you're poorly yourself, then write down on a piece of paper what it is you want, and the rabbi will read it and say a prayer for you!"

"No, I must see him!"

"Can you come back after the holidays?"

"I'm afraid I can't. I must see him today!"

"In that case, I can't help you. You'd better go through the kitchen!"

"Where is the kitchen?"

"Around the other side."

"Around the other side" there was a gentleman waiting who had evidently paid out a lot of money. He was a gentleman, in every respect a gentleman. You could tell that by his girth, his fur coat, and the expression of his eyes, which were not looking for anything to look at and had not found anything. He knew exactly that the kitchen door would open in five minutes, ten at the latest.

But when the door did open, the rich gentleman turned rather pale. We walked along a dark passageway that had an uneven floor, and the gentleman struck matches and still walked a little apprehensively.

He was with the rabbi for a long time, and came out in a high good humor. I heard later that the gentleman had the sensible habit of going to see the rabbi by the kitchen route every year, that he was a rich naphtha merchant and mine owner, and that he scattered so much money among the poor that he was allowed to duck out of many of his obligations without needing to fear a fine.

The rabbi sat in a plain room, at a small table in front of a window that looked out over a courtyard, with his left elbow resting on the table. He had black hair, a short black beard, and gray eyes. His nose jutted powerfully from his face, as though on a sudden impulse, widening and flattening a little at the tip. The rabbi's hands were bony and thin, and his fingers had sharp white nails.

He asked in a clear voice what I had come about, cast a quick look in my direction, and then gazed out into the courtyard again.

I replied that I had heard much about his wisdom and had wanted to meet him.

"God is wise!" he said, and looked at me again.

He beckoned to me to come to the table, shook my hand, and, with the heartfelt tone of an old friend, bade me: "Farewell!"

I left the same way I had come. In the kitchen the red-haired man was hurriedly eating a bowl of bean soup with a wooden spoon. I gave him a banknote. He took it in his left hand, continuing to ply his spoon with his right.

Outside he caught up with me. He wanted to hear what news I had, wondered whether the Japanese were once again preparing for war.[*]

We talked about wars and about Europe. He said: "I have heard that the Japanese are not *goyim* like the Europeans. Why then are they making war?"

Any Japanese, I think, would have had difficulty answering his question.

I SAW that there were many red-haired Jews living in the little town. A few weeks later they celebrated the Feast of the Torah, and I watched them dance. It wasn't the dance of a degenerate race. It was more than the energy given by a fanatical faith. It was a kind of health that took the occasion to break out into religion.

The hasidim took each other by the hand, they danced in a ring, broke up the ring and clapped their hands, they

[*]Probably a reference to the Russo-Japanese War of 1904–5.

tossed their heads left and right in time to the music, they picked up their Torah scrolls and swung them around like partners, clasped them to their bosom, and kissed them and shed tears of joy. There was eroticism in their dance. It moved me deeply to see a whole people that didn't separate physical cravings from spiritual joys but united them, consecrating its sensual pleasure to its God, making the book that contained its strictest laws into a beloved. There was fervor and ardor together, dancing as a form of worship, an orgy of prayer.

The people drank mead from great tankards. Who is responsible for the lie that Jews don't drink? It's the expression, half admiring, half reproachful, of suspicion of a people who are accused of being unremittingly conscious. But I saw Jews losing consciousness, admittedly not after three pints of beer but after five tankards of strong mead, and not on the anniversary of a battle but out of joy that God had chosen to share his knowledge and his law with them.

I HAD seen them losing consciousness once before, but that was through prayer. It was during Yom Kippur. In Western Europe that gets translated as the "Day of Atonement," a phrase that reflects the Western Jew's whole willingness to compromise. But Yom Kippur is a day not of atonement but of expiation, a heavy day whose twenty-four hours contain enough penitence for twenty-four years. It begins at four o'clock the previous afternoon. In an almost entirely Jewish town, this greatest of all Jewish festivals feels just as a great tempest must feel to those in a frail vessel on the high seas. The streets suddenly go dark as candlelight breaks from windows, and the shutters are closed in fearful haste—and so tightly closed that one has the impression they won't be opened again until Judgment Day. There is a general taking leave of all worldly things: of business, of joy, of nature, of food, of the street and the family, of friends and acquaintances. People who just two hours ago walked the public streets in their everyday clothes, wearing ordinary expressions, hasten through the lanes quite transformed, making for the prayerhouse, dressed in the heavy black silk and dread white of their funeral suits, in white socks and loose slippers, head down, their prayer-coats bundled under their arms. The great silence that now deafens an otherwise almost orientally noisy town oppresses even the lively children, whose shouting and crying play such a prominent part in the symphony of the streets. All the fathers now bless their children. All the women now weep in front of the silver candelabra. All friends embrace one another. All enemies beg one another for forgiveness. The choir of angels blows a fanfare for Judgment Day. Soon Jehovah will open the great volume in which this year's sins, punishments, and destinies are recorded. Candles burn now for all the dead. Other candles are lit for the living. The dead are only one step away from this world, as the living are from the next.

The great praying begins. The great fasting has been in progress for an hour already. Hundreds, thousands, tens of thousands of candles burn behind or beside one another, they incline together, they pool in one great flame. From a thousand windows there breaks a wailing prayer, interspersed by soft, mild, otherworldly melodies copied from those of heaven. In all the prayerhouses, the people stand, crowded together. Some prostrate themselves on the ground, lie there for a long time, then get up, sit on footstools or flagstones, hunker there, and suddenly leap to their feet, sway back and forth from the waist, and run around incessantly in the tiny space like ecstatic sentries of prayer. Entire buildings are filled with white funeral shirts, with the living who are absent, with the dead who are alive. Not a single drop is permitted to moisten the parched lips and refresh the dry throats that cry out in so much pain—not to the world but to the heavens. They will not break their fast today or tomorrow. It is a shocking thing to know that not one Jew in this town is going to eat or drink. All have suddenly turned into spirits, with the attributes of spirits. Every little trader is somehow superhuman, because this is the day on which he wants to reach God. All stretch out their hands to touch the hem of his garment. All without distinction: The rich are no better off than the poor, as none of them will have anything to eat. All are sinners, and all pray. A giddiness comes over them, they reel, they rant, they whisper, they hurt themselves; they sing, shout, wail. Heavy tears trickle down their old beards, and their hunger is taken away by so much pain in their souls and by the immemorial melodies that fill their ecstatic ears.

THE ONLY comparable transformation I saw was at a Jewish funeral.

The body of the devout Jew lies in a plain wooden box, covered with a black cloth. It is not wheeled but carried, by four Jews running at a brisk clip along the shortest possible way—I'm not sure whether this is part of the ceremonial or because a slower walk would double the weight for the bearers. They almost race through the town with the corpse. The preparations have taken a day. A body is not allowed to remain unburied for more than twenty-four hours. The wailing of the mourners can be heard all over town. The women run through the streets, crying out their grief to every stranger. They talk to the deceased, call him by his pet names, beg him for mercy and forgiveness, reproach themselves terribly, and ask in bewilderment what they will do without him. They declare that they want to die—and all while running down the middle of the public street—as indifferent faces peer out from windows and other people go about their business, carts trundle by, and shopkeepers offer their wares.

The most shattering scenes take place at the cemetery. Women refuse to leave the graves; they have to be dragged away; they require taming as much as comfort-

ing. The melody for the prayer for the dead is of a mon-
umental plainness, the burial ceremony is almost curt in
its brevity. Great crowds of beggars scrap for alms.

For seven days the mourners sit in the house of the
departed, on the floor, on little stools, walking around in
stockinged feet, themselves half dead. In the windows a
small, dim light burns in front of a piece of white linen,
and the neighbors bring the mourners a hard-boiled
egg, suitable food for those whose pain is round, with no
beginning and no end.

BUT JOY can be just as violent as sorrow.

A wonder-rabbi was marrying his fourteen-year-old
son to the sixteen-year-old daughter of a colleague, and
both rabbis' hasidim came to the celebrations, which
lasted for eight days, with six hundred guests.

The authorities had given them the use of an old,
derelict barracks. The guests were on the road for three
days. They came with carts, horses, sacks of straw, pillows,
children, jewelry, and large trunks. They settled into rooms
in the barracks.

There was a great commotion in the little town. A
couple of hundred hasidim put on old Russian costumes,
buckled on old swords, and rode into town bareback.
There were some good riders among them, and they gave
the lie to all the bad jokes about Jewish army doctors, in
which Jews are said to be afraid of horses.

It went on for eight days—the noise, the crowds, the singing and dancing and drinking. I was not admitted to the celebration. It had been put on for the participants and their guests. Strangers milled around outside, peered through the windows, and listened to the dance music, which, in case you were wondering, was good.

Because there are good Jewish musicians in the East. Music is another hereditary profession. Some musicians earn great respect and a local reputation. The true musicians among them have no greater ambition than that. Unable to write music, they compose melodies that they hand on to their sons and sometimes to great parts of the Eastern Jewish people. They compose its folk music. After their deaths, anecdotes about their lives may make the rounds for a further fifty years. Then their names are forgotten, while their tunes continue to be sung and gradually make their way through the world.

The musicians are very poor, because they live off the joys of strangers. They are paid a pittance and are glad if they are allowed to take leftover tidbits and cakes back to their families. They receive tips from the rich guests for whom they play. Following the ineluctable law of the East, every poor man, including therefore the musician, has numerous children. In the musician's case this is both good and bad, for the sons will go on to be musicians in turn, and form a "band," which, the bigger it is, the more money it will earn. The more people who bear the family name, the more the band's renown will grow. Sometimes a later descendant of this family will go out into the world, and become a celebrated virtuoso. There are a few such now living in the West; it would serve no purpose to name them. Not because it might somehow embarrass them, but because it would be unfair to their unknown ancestors, who don't need to have their greatness confirmed by any talented descendants.

Artistic fame also attaches to the singers—the precentors, or cantors as they are called in the West—known professionally as *hazanim*. These singers tend to fare better than the musicians, because their appointed task is a religious one and their art is sacred and liturgical. They are up alongside the priest. A few, whose reputation has spread as far as the United States, receive invitations to perform in the wealthy Jewish neighborhoods there. In Paris, which has several wealthy Eastern Jewish congregations, the representatives of the synagogues like to invite one of the celebrated singers and cantors from the East every year for the High Holy Days. Then the Jews attend prayers in the same spirit as one might attend a concert, and have their spiritual and artistic needs satisfied at once. It may be that the content of the many sung prayers and the spaces in which they are heard heighten the artistic reputation of the singer. I have never been able to verify whether those Jews were right who insisted to me that such and such a *hazan* was better than Caruso.

THE ODDEST PROFESSION is that of the *batlan*, the Eastern Jewish joker, a fool, a philosopher, a storyteller. Each shtetl has at least one *batlan*. He entertains the guests at weddings and bar mitzvahs. He sleeps in the prayerhouse, dreams up stories, listens to the men arguing, and racks his brain about all kinds of useless matters. No one takes him seriously. But he is the most serious person imaginable. He could have dealt in feathers or coral just as well as the prosperous merchant who invites him to a wedding in order to laugh at him. But he doesn't trade. To work, to marry, to have children, to become a respected member of society—all these seem beyond him. Sometimes he treks from village to village, from town to town. He doesn't starve, but he's always on the brink of starvation. He doesn't perish, he goes hungry, but he wants to go hungry. His stories would probably cause a stir in Europe if they were published. Many of them deal with subjects that are familiar from Yiddish and Russian literature. The famous Shalom Aleichem was a typical *batlan*—only with greater ambition, sense of purpose, and awareness of his cultural mission.

A narrative gift is something frequently found in the East. In every family there is an uncle who is good at telling stories. They are like oral novelists, elaborating their stories beforehand, or else improvising them in the telling.

The winter nights are long and cold, and the storytellers, who often don't have enough firewood, are happy to tell stories in return for a few glasses of hot tea and a place by the stove. They are treated differently—better— than the professional jokers, because they at least attempt to follow a practical profession, and are clever enough, in the presence of a typical, level-headed Jew, to conceal the beautiful madness that the fools blazon out. The fools are revolutionaries. The amateur storytellers have concluded compromises with the workaday world and have remained dilettantes. The average Jew thinks of philosophy and art as mere "entertainment"—unless they have a religious dimension. At least he's honest enough to admit it, and doesn't air his views on music or painting.

In recent years the Yiddish theater has become so widely known in the West that a description here would be superfluous. It's become almost more of an institution of the Western ghetto than the East. The religious Jew does not attend it, in the belief that it offends against religious laws. The theater audiences in the East are enlightened Jews, who generally have nationalist sympathies by now. They are Europeans, though still a world away from the sort of Western European theatergoer who purposes nothing more than to "kill an evening."

THE RUSTIC JEW of Eastern Europe is a type completely unknown in the West. No wonder: He has never gotten there. No less "a son of the soil" than the peasant, he is half peasant himself. He is a sharecropper or a miller or a village innkeeper. He has never learned a trade. Often he is completely illiterate. At most he is capable of doing little deals. He's barely any cleverer than the peasant. He is big and strong and of an improbably sound constitution. He is physically brave, doesn't mind a fistfight, and is afraid of nothing. Many take advantage of their superiority to the peasants, something that provoked local pogroms in old Russia and anti-Semitic campaigns in Galicia. But many are of a peasantlike meekness and greatheartedness. Many have the healthy common sense that one tends to find in the countryside, and that develops wherever a sensible race is immediately subject to the laws of nature.

It is difficult for me to talk about the Eastern Jewish proletariat. I am unable to exonerate a great part of this proletariat from the grave charge of being opposed to its own class; and if not opposed, then at least indifferent. None of the many untrue and unjust accusations that are brought against Eastern Jews by the West are as untrue and unjust as the accusation that they are what the gutter press likes to call Bolshevik. Of all the world's poor, the poor Jew is surely the most conservative. He practically underwrites the perpetuation of the old social order. The great mass of the Jews are an overwhelmingly bourgeois class with separate national, religious, and racial traits. Anti-Semitism in the East (and in the West too, for that matter) is often more revolutionary, being, as the saying goes, "a socialism for idiots"—but a form of socialism nonetheless. The poor Slav, the peasant, the worker, the artisan—all of them live in the conviction that the Jew has money. He has as little money as his anti-Semitic enemies. But he lives respectably. He starves and stints himself in a more methodical way than the Christian proletarian does. You might say: He misses his meals at more regular hours. Only once a week—on Friday night—does he eat like his better-off coreligionists. He sends his children to school, where they wear better clothes; he is able to save a little money; and, being from an ancient line, he always has some possession or other: some piece of jewelry handed down to him, a bed, some furniture. He can always lay his hand on some valuable in his house. He is smart enough not to sell anything. He doesn't drink, and he doesn't have the sad, but healthy frivolity or indiscipline of the Christian workingman. He is always in a position to give his daughter a trousseau, and almost always a small dowry as well. He can even afford to keep a son-in-law. Whether the Jew is an artisan or a small trader, a poor scholar or temple-servant, a beggar or a water carrier—he *refuses* to be a proletarian. He *insists* on maintaining a distinction between himself and the country's poor. He *plays* at being a little better off than he is. If he is a beggar, he would rather go cap in hand to the houses of the rich than stay in the street. And if he does beg in the street, then his main income is from a kind of principal supplier, whom he looks up with the utmost punctuality. He won't beg from the richer farmer, but from the less-well-off Jew he will. He keeps a kind of middle-class self-respect. The Jews' bourgeois propensity for charitable giving has its roots in the conservatism of Judaism, and it gets in the way of the radicalization of the Jewish proletariat. Religion and morals rule out all forms of violence, rule out agitation, incitement, and even the public display of envy. The poor devout Jew is reconciled to his destiny as much as the poor believer of any other religion. God makes one man rich, the other poor. Incitement against the rich would be tantamount to incitement against God.

The only consciously proletarian Jew is the Jewish worker. He tends to espouse socialism of various hues. The Eastern Jewish proletarian is thereby less of a Jew than his bourgeois or semiproletarian coreligionists are. Less of a Jew, even if he is a Jewish nationalist and Zionist. The most nationalistic Jewish socialist is the Poal Zionist, who aspires toward a socialist, or at least a workers', state of Palestine. The boundaries between Jewish socialists and communists are less clear-cut than they are elsewhere, and there can be no talk of a German-style riven proletariat. Many Jewish workers belong to the Socialist or Communist Parties of their respective countries, which makes them Polish, Russian, or Romanian Socialists. Social issues almost invariably take precedence over national ones. It's how workers of all countries see things. "National self-determination" is an intellectual luxury for a group that has nothing more serious to worry about. If there is one nation that is justified in seeing the "national question" as essential to its survival, then surely it is the Jews, who are forced to become a "nation" by the nationalism of the others. But the workers of *this* nation still sense the greater urgency of social issues. Their identification with the proletariat is stronger, more honest, and more consequent: They are "more radical," which, in the vocabulary of the party-barons in Western Europe seems to have become a negative attribute. But it is merely a mistake on the part of the anti-Semites to suppose that Jews are radical revolutionaries. To middle- and lower-middle-class Jews, the idea of the Jewish revolutionary is an abomination.

I am put in the embarrassing position of having to call people proletarian against their own wishes. In a minority of cases I can soften the blow by nonsensically dubbing them—the term was invented in Western Europe—"white-collar proletarians." Among these I would include Torah scribes, Jewish teachers, the makers of prayer shawls and producers of candles, the ritual butchers and the little religious officials. We can call them members of a religious proletariat. But beyond them there is a vast crowd of sufferers, oppressed and despised, comforted neither by faith nor by class consciousness nor by revolutionary enthusiasm. Among them are the water carriers in the shtetl, who, from early morning till late at night, fill the water barrels in the homes of the better-off in return for a minimal weekly wage. They are touchingly naive people, of an almost un-Jewish physical strength. On the same rung of the social ladder are the furniture movers, the porters, and a whole lot of others who live from occasional work, but always from physical labor. They are healthy, brave, and good-hearted. I don't know of any people in whom goodness is situated so close to physical strength, or rudeness so far removed from a coarse occupation, as with the Jewish day laborer.

Some Slav peasants who converted to Judaism also live by such casual labor. Such conversions are relatively frequent in the East, even though official Judaism opposes them, and of all the religions in the world the Jewish faith is the one that doesn't set out to make converts. No question, the Eastern Jews have a much greater admixture of Slav blood in their veins than the German Jews have of German. So when Western European anti-Semites and German Jews claim that Eastern Jews are "more Semitic" and hence "more dangerous," they are as mistaken as the Western Jewish banker who feels himself "more Aryan" on the strength of mixed marriages that have taken place in his family.

GHETTOES IN THE WEST

VIENNA

I.

The Eastern Jews who come to Vienna settle in the Leopoldstadt, the second of the twenty districts. There, they are close to the Prater and the Nordbahnhof. Peddlers can make a living in the Prater—from selling picture postcards to tourists and from the compassion that happily often accompanies pleasure-seeking. The Nordbahnhof, meanwhile, is where they all arrived. The scents of home still waft through its lofty halls, and it remains the gateway for their possible return.

The Leopoldstadt is a sort of voluntary ghetto. Many bridges connect it to other parts of the city. Every day, the traders, peddlers, brokers, and deal makers—all the unproductive elements of immigrant Jewry—may be seen funneling across these bridges. But these same bridges are also crossed by the progeny of said unproductive elements, the sons and daughters of the traders, who work in factories, offices, editorial suites, and workshops.

The sons and daughters of Eastern Jews are productive. Their parents may be hawkers and peddlers, but among the younger generation are many of the most gifted lawyers, doctors, bankers, journalists, and actors.

The Leopoldstadt is a poor district. There are tiny apartments that house families of six. There are tiny hostels where fifty or sixty bed down on the floors.

The Prater is where the homeless live rough. The very poorest workers live in the vicinity of the station. The Eastern Jews don't live any better than the Christian inhabitants of this district.

They have lots of children, they are unaccustomed to hygiene and cleanliness. They are detested.

No one will do anything for them. Their cousins and coreligionists, with their feet safely pushed under desks in the First District, have already gone "native." They don't want to be associated with Eastern Jews, much less taken for them. The Christian Socialist and German Nationalist Parties both have anti-Semitism as an important plank of their political programs. The Social Democrats are wary of being thought a "Jewish party." The Jewish nationalists are fairly impotent. In any case they are a middle-class outfit, and the great mass of Eastern Jews are working class.

The Eastern Jews depend on the support of middle-class charitable organizations. People are inclined to rate

Jewish compassion more highly than it deserves. In fact Jewish charity is just as imperfect an institution as any other. First and foremost charity benefits the giver. In a Jewish welfare office the Eastern Jew often finds himself treated no better by his coreligionists or fellow nationals than by Christians. It is terribly hard to be an Eastern Jew; there is no harder lot than that of the Eastern Jew newly arrived in Vienna.

2.

When he sets foot in the Second District, he is greeted by familiar faces. Or do they really greet him? No, he probably just sees them. People who have already been there for ten years have no use for the recent arrival. Someone else has arrived. Someone else wants to earn. Someone else wants to live.

The worst of it is: He can't just be left to perish. He's not a stranger. He is a Jew and a compatriot.

Someone will be found to take him in. Someone else will advance him a small loan or get him credit. Someone else will organize a territory for him, or turn over his own. The new arrival will go into installment selling.

His first and most difficult call is on the police.

The man behind the counter dislikes Jews in general, and Eastern Jews in particular.

He will demand to see papers. Exotic, improbable

papers. Papers the like of which are never required from
Christian immigrants. Besides, Christian papers are in
order. All Christians have sensible, European names. Jewish names are mad and Jewish. Nor is that all: They have
two or three surnames, qualified by *false* or *recte*. You never
know what to call them. Their parents were married by a
rabbi. The marriage has no legal standing. If the father's
name is Weinstock, and the mother's Abramovsky, then
the children of their union will be called Weinstock *recte*
Abramovsky, or perhaps Abramovsky *false* Weinstock. The
boy, for example, is given the Jewish first name of Leib
Nachman. Because the name is difficult and might sound
provocative to others' ears, the son styles himself Leo. So
his name is: Leib Nachman, styled Leo Abramovsky *false*
Weinstock.

As far as the police are concerned, names like that
are nothing but trouble. The police don't like trouble. Nor
is it just the names. The birthdates are inaccurate. The
papers have generally been burned. (The registry offices
in small towns in Galicia, Lithuania, and Ukraine were
continually ablaze.) All the papers have been lost. Nationality is a moot point. Following the War and the Treaty of
Versailles, it's become still more complicated. Now, how
did our man get across the border? Without a passport?
Or with a false one? That means his name isn't his real
name—even though he gave so many of them, so many, in
fact, that they can't all be right—but it's probably wrong
in an objective sense as well. The man listed on the papers,

on the alien registration form, isn't the same as the man who's standing in front of him. So what's to be done? Lock him up? Then the wrong man would be locked up. Have him extradited? That would be extraditing an imposter. Whereas if he's told to come back with proper papers, with sensible names on them, then it wouldn't just be sending the right man packing, but maybe a way of making a wrong'un into a proper one.

So he's sent packing, and again, and again, and again. Till it dawns on the Jew that he has no option but to give false information for the correct impression. To stick to one name that might not be his but would be a plausible and believable name anyway. The police have given the Eastern Jew the idea of concealing a true but tangled set of circumstances behind bogus but tidy ones.

Everyone professes astonishment at the capacity of Jews to give false information. No one professes astonishment at the naive expectations of the police.

3.

The two career alternatives are peddler and installment seller.

A peddler carries a selection of soaps, suspenders, rubber goods, buttons, and pencils around in a basket strapped to his back. With that little portable shop on board, he calls on various cafés and restaurants. It's advisable to think beforehand whether one will be welcome in a certain establishment or not.

To be a reasonably successful peddler also requires years of experience. The best bet is to go of an evening to Piowati's, where the well-off clientele dunk kosher sausages in horseradish. Even the owner owes it to the Jewish reputation of his business to offer the peddler a bowl of soup. That's a start. So far as the customers are concerned, if they are already full, they may be in a pleasantly benevolent frame of mind. Nowhere is kindness so intimately related to physical well-being as with the Jewish merchant. When he has eaten, and eaten well, he is even capable of buying suspenders, though he may stock them in his own shop. Generally, though, he won't buy anything and will just give the peddler a small coin.

Of course, one should take care not to be the sixth peddler on a given evening to turn up at Piowati's. Kindness tends to be exhausted after about three. I knew a Jewish hawker once who called on the same branch of Piowati's at three-hour intervals. He had figured out that that was when the generations of eaters tended to succeed one another. If there was still the odd guest left from the previous sitting, the hawker was careful to avoid his table. He knew precisely where the boundary between generosity and irritation lay.

At a certain stage of drunkenness, even Christians may be kind-hearted. One may set foot in little local bars and cafés on a Sunday without fear. One will be teased a little and called names, but it's all in good part. The more humorous individuals will take away one's basket and hide it, and generally drive the hawker to the brink of despair. But *nil desperandum*! These are nothing but expressions of the golden hearts of the Viennese. When it's all done and dusted, he'll be able to sell a picture postcard or two.

All his earnings will not be sufficient to feed him. Nevertheless the peddler will be able to keep a wife and children. He will send his children to middle school if they are gifted, and by the grace of God they are gifted. His son will one day become a famous lawyer, but the father who had to spend so much of his life as a peddler will want to go on peddling. Sometimes it transpires that the peddler's great-grandchildren will be anti-Semitic Christian Socialists. These things happen.

4.

What is the difference between a peddler and an installment salesman? The former sells things for cash, and the latter on installment. The former requires a small "network" of clientele, and the latter an extended one. The former will only take the commuter railway, whereas the latter goes out on the city-to-city routes. The former will never make a businessman; the latter may.

An installment seller is only viable in a time of stable currency. The great Inflation drove all the installment sellers out of their sorry business.* They became money changers.

A money changer fared little better. When he bought Romanian leis, the rate went down. When he sold, it rose. When the dollar was high in Berlin and the mark was high in Vienna, he went to Berlin to buy marks. He returned to Vienna to buy dollars with the high mark. Then he took his dollars to Berlin to buy yet more marks. But no locomotive can keep pace with a falling mark. By the time he was back in Vienna, he had half what he set out with.

In order to make money the currency dealer would have to be in telephone contact with money markets all over the world. However, all he was in contact with was the black market where he was. Both the harmful effects and the connections of the black market have been greatly exaggerated. Blacker by far than the black market was the official exchange—innocent, whiter than white, and enjoying police protection. The black market was the dirty competition to an institution that was itself dirty. The currency dealers were whipping boys for the so-called honorable banks.

Only a handful of small currency dealers can ever have gotten rich.

Today most of them are what they were before: poor installment sellers.

---

*During the great Inflation of 1923, money lost so much in value that it was carted around in wheelbarrows and used for papering walls.

5.

The installment seller's customers are people with an income but no money. Students, petty officials, workers. Every week the installment seller makes the rounds of his customers to collect payments and make new sales. Since the needs of these little people are great, they buy a lot, relatively speaking. Since their incomes are very low, they pay little, relatively speaking. The installment seller is never sure whether to be pleased about new sales or not. The more he sells, the longer it will be till he gets his money.

What if he put up his prices? Then people will just go to the nearest department store; by now even small towns have them. The installment seller is cheaper for them, because he pays the train fare, which otherwise they would have to pay. With him they get the department store in their homes. He is more convenient.

And so life for him is inconvenient. If he wants to save on the train fare, he will have to go on foot, heavily laden. So it takes him a long time. He doesn't get where he needs to get on time. On Sunday he needs to call on all the customers who owe him money. Saturday is payday, but by Monday they'll be broke again. If the installment seller does take the train, it will cost him. He will get where he needs to get to, but often enough his customers will have blown their wages by Sunday anyway.

These are the occupational hazards of being a Jew.

6.

What other possibilities are open to an Eastern Jew? If he's a worker, no factory will employ him. There are enough local people out of work. But even if there weren't—they wouldn't hire a Christian foreigner, let alone a Jew.

There are also Eastern Jewish artisans. Many Eastern Jewish tailors live in Leopoldstadt and Brigittenau. Jews are gifted tailors. But there's quite a difference between having premises—a "fashion salon" even—in the Herrengasse, in the First District, and a workshop in the kitchen of a tenement in the Kleine Schiffgasse.

Whoever comes to the Kleine Schiffgasse? Anyone who's not forced to go there would sooner pass it by. The Kleine Schiffgasse smells of onions and kerosene, herrings and soap, dishwater and rubbish, petroleum and cooking, mold and delicatessen. Dirty children play in the Kleine Schiffgasse. Carpets are beaten and featherbeds aired in its open windows. Goosedown drifts in the air.

In such a street lives the little Jewish tailor. If only it were just a matter of the street! His apartment consists of one room and a kitchen. And, according to the puzzling laws which God has established for the Jews, a poor Jewish tailor will have half a dozen children and only rarely an assistant. The sewing machine clatters, the iron is parked on the chopping board, he sits on the marriage bed to measure up his customers. Who would seek out such a tailor?

You really can't claim that the Eastern Jewish tailor "sucks on the marrow of the native population." He doesn't take any trade away from a Christian tailor. He's an expert at cutting fabric, his work is first-rate. Maybe in twenty years' time he really will have a fashion salon in the Herrengasse, in the First District. If he does he will have earned it. Eastern Jews are no magicians. Anything they may achieve costs them effort, sweat, and hunger.

7.

If an Eastern Jew has money and a lot of luck, he may be able, under certain circumstances, to purchase a "concession" and open a shop. It will be patronized by the poor people of the district. For instance the tailor described above. He wouldn't pay cash, he would receive credit. That's how an Eastern Jew "does business."

There are Eastern Jewish intellectuals. Teachers, scribes, and so forth. And there are some who live on handouts. Shamefaced beggars. Panhandlers. Musicians. Newspaper vendors. Even bootblacks.

And so-called "air sellers." Traders in "air goods." The wares are at a station in Hungary somewhere. Or then again, perhaps not. But they are sold on the Franz Joseph Quay in Vienna.

There are Eastern Jewish swindlers and crooks. Yes, I said it: crooks! But then I have heard there are Western European crooks, too.

8.

The two principal streets of Leopoldstadt are the Taborstrasse and the Praterstrasse. The Praterstrasse is almost elegant. It leads to the Prater and pleasure. It is peopled by Jews and Christians. It is smooth, wide, and bright. There are plenty of cafés on it.

There are a lot of cafés on the Taborstrasse too. They are Jewish cafés. Their owners are largely Jewish, their clientele is Jewish almost to a man. Jews like to go to cafés to read the paper, to play tarock and chess, to do deals.

Jews are gifted chess players. Sometimes they play against Christian opponents. A good Christian chess player is not likely to be an anti-Semite.

There are many standing customers in Jewish cafés. They are a "casual public" in the true sense. They are regulars without taking food or drink there. They will drop into a café eighteen times a morning. They have to, for business.

They make a lot of noise. Their voices are loud and penetrating and uninhibited. Because all the customers are well-mannered and cosmopolitan, no one attracts special attention, though they are all striking enough.

In a true Jewish café you can walk in with your head under your arm and no one will notice.

9.

The war caused a lot of Jewish refugees to come to Vienna. For as long as their homelands were occupied, they were entitled to "support." Not that money was sent to them where they were. They had to stand in line for it on the coldest winter days, and into the night. All of them: old people, invalids, women, and children.

They took to smuggling. They brought flour, meat, and eggs from Hungary. They were locked up in Hungary for buying up foodstocks. They were locked up in Austria for importing unrationed foodstuffs. They made life easier for the Viennese. They were locked up for it.

When the war was over, they were repatriated, sometimes forcibly. A Social Democratic provincial governor had them thrown out. To Christian Socialists, they are Jews. To German nationalists, they are Semitic. To Social Democrats, they are unproductive elements.

What they are is out-of-work proletarians. A peddler is a member of the proletariat.

If he's not allowed to work with his hands, he works with his feet. It's not his fault if he can't find a better job. What's the use of all these truisms? Who believes truisms anyway?

BERLIN

I.

No Eastern Jew goes to Berlin voluntarily. Who in all the world goes to Berlin voluntarily?

Berlin is a point of transit, where, given compelling reasons, one may end up staying longer. Berlin has no ghetto. It has a Jewish district. This is where emigrants come who want to get to America via Hamburg or Amsterdam. This is where they often get stuck. They haven't enough money. Or their papers are not in order.

(Again: papers! Half a Jew's life is consumed by the futile battle with papers.)

The Eastern Jews who come to Berlin are often on a transit visa that allows them to stay in Germany for two to three days. There are quite a few who came on a transit visa, and end up staying in Berlin for two or three years.

Berlin has long-established Eastern Jews, who generally arrived before the War. Their relatives came after them. Refugees from the occupied lands came to Berlin. Jews who had served in the German armies of occupation in Russia, Ukraine, Poland, and Lithuania had to return to Germany with the German army.

There are Eastern Jewish criminals in Berlin as well. Pickpockets, bigamists and con artists, counterfeiters, racketeers. Hardly any burglars. No violent criminals, no murderers.

The struggle for papers, the struggle against papers, is something an Eastern Jew gets free of only if he uses criminal methods to take on society. The Eastern Jewish criminal was generally a criminal in his past life. He gets to Germany on false papers, or with none at all. He doesn't register with the police.

Only the honest Eastern Jew—honest and timorous—registers with the police. It's much more difficult in Prussia than in Austria. The Berlin police like to undertake house-to-house searches. They check papers on the streets as well. They did a lot of that during the Inflation.

The trade in secondhand clothes is not prohibited, but it's not sanctioned either. No one without a hawker's license is allowed to buy my old trousers. Or sell them, for that matter.

But buy them he does. And sells them too. He stands on the Joachimsthaler Strasse, or on the corner of Joachimsthaler and the Kurfürstendamm, pretending to mind his own business. He has to be able to tell from the look of a passerby, first, whether he has old clothes to sell, and second, if he needs money.

Whatever clothes he manages to buy, he sells the next morning at the old-clothes exchange.

There are distinctions among hawkers too. There are rich and powerful hawkers, to whom the little ones look up shyly and humbly. The more money a hawker has, the more he earns. He doesn't go out on the street himself anymore. He doesn't need to. I'm not even sure whether it is still appropriate to refer to him as a "hawker." In fact he has a secondhand clothes shop and a business license. The license is not in his own name but that of someone settled in Berlin, a solid citizen who doesn't know anything about clothes but takes a cut from the business all the same.

The clothing exchange is where the hawkers and shop owners do business in the mornings. The former bring along yesterday's crop of old dresses and jackets. In spring, light garments and sporty clothes are at a premium. In autumn, it's tailcoats, dinner jackets, and striped trousers. Anyone who comes along with linen suits and summer clothes in the autumn is in the wrong business.

The clothes that the hawker has bought from pas-sersby for pathetic sums are sold to the shopkeeper at a ridiculous markup. The shopkeeper then has them pressed and mended, and generally "freshened up." Then he hangs them outside his shop to flutter in the breeze.

Anyone who is good at selling old clothes will soon graduate to selling new clothes. He will go from a shop to a fashion store. Someday, he will have his own department store.

It is possible for a hawker to make a career in Berlin. He will assimilate faster there than his equivalent would in Vienna. Berlin levels out differences and kills off particularities. Hence the lack of a Jewish ghetto there.

There are just a couple of small Jewish streets around the Warschauer Brücke and in the Scheunenviertel. The most Jewish street in Berlin is the melancholy Hirtenstrasse.

2.

The Hirtenstrasse is the saddest street in the world. It doesn't even have the unreflective joy of real dirt.

The Hirtenstrasse is a Berlin street, softened perhaps by its Eastern Jewish inhabitants, but fundamentally unchanged. It has no streetcar line, no buses, only rarely an automobile; mostly just trucks, carts, the most functional and plebeian of conveyances. There are little hole-in-the-wall bars. You climb a few steps to reach them. Narrow, filthy, worn-out steps. The step equivalent of down-at-heel shoes. Rubbish is piled up in the doorways of houses. Sometimes this rubbish is collectible, even marketable. Rubbish as stock-in-trade. Old newspapers. Torn stockings. Widowed soles. Shoelaces. Apron strings. The Hirtenstrasse is drab like a slum. It lacks the character of a street in a shtetl. It has a new, cheap, already-used-up, bargain-basement quality. A street out of a department store. A cheap department store. It has one or two dirty window displays. Jewish bakeries, poppyseed cakes, rolls, rye loaves. An oil canister, sweating flypaper.

In addition, it has Jewish Talmud schools and prayer-houses. You see Hebrew writing. It looks out of place on these walls. You see the spines of books behind sullied windows.

You see Jews walking, with their tallith under their arms. Emerging from the prayerhouse, going about their business. You see sick children and old women.

There are repeated attempts to transform this boring Berlinish semisanitized street into a ghetto. But Berlin is always stronger. The residents fight an unavailing fight. They want to spread out? Berlin repeatedly presses them back.

3.

I step inside one of the small bars. There are a few customers waiting for lunch in the back room. They have their hats on. The landlady is standing between the kitchen and the public bar. Her husband stands behind the counter. He has a beard made out of red thread. He seems apprehensive.

And why shouldn't he be apprehensive? Don't the police pay him visits? Haven't they been there several times lately? The landlord shakes hands with me just in case. And just in case, he says: "Oh, such a customer! Has it really been so long since you last did us the honor?" A warm greeting never hurts.

Everyone drinks the classic Jewish beverage—mead. That's the alcohol on which they can get intoxicated. They love the heavy, dark brown mead, sweet, crisp, and strong.

4.

From time to time the "Temple of Solomon" makes an appearance in Berlin. This temple has been put together by one Herr Frohmann from Drohobycz in exact accordance with the description in the Bible, only using balsa and papier-mâché and gold paint instead of the cedarwood and real gold of King Solomon.

Frohmann claims to have spent seven years building this minitemple, and I believe him. To build a model temple in accordance with the description in the Bible must cost as much labor as love.

Every single curtain, courtyard, crenellation, and altarpiece is plainly visible. The temple is on a table in the backroom of a bar. There is a smell of gefilte fish. Very few visitors come and look. The old folks are already familiar with it, and the young people want to go to Palestine and build roads, not temples.

And Frohmann travels from ghetto to ghetto, from Jew to Jew, showing off his creation. Frohmann is the guardian of tradition and of the only great architectonic work that the Jews have ever produced, and for that reason will never forget. To me Frohmann is an expression of longing, of the longing of an entire people. I saw an old Jew standing in front of the miniature temple. He was no different from his brethren who stand before the one sacred remaining wall of the real ruined temple, weeping and praying.[*]

5.

I stumbled upon the cabaret by chance, wandering through the dark streets on a bright evening, looking through the windows of small prayerhouses, which by day were no more than shopfronts, but in the morning and evening, houses of worship. The Jews of the East maintain a close proximity between commerce and heaven; all they need for worship is ten adult—older than thirteen— members of their faith, a cantor, and a knowledge of the cardinal points, so that they can identify *Misrach*, the East, the Holy Land, the source of light.

[*] The Wailing Wall in Jerusalem.

Hereabouts everything is improvised: The temple is people coming together, trade is stopping in the middle of the street. Basically, it is still the flight out of Egypt, which has been in progress now for thousands of years. The people always have to be on the alert, be packed and ready, have a piece of bread and an onion in one pocket and the *tefillim* in the other. Who can say whether he won't have to resume his wanderings in another hour? Even theater happens suddenly.

The cabaret I saw was set up in the yard of a dirty old inn. It was a rectangular, glassed-in yard, whose walls were windows, giving onto corridors and passages, revealing such domestic details as beds, shirts, and buckets. A stray linden tree stood in the middle of it, representing nature. Through one or two lit-up windows you could see inside the kitchen of a kosher restaurant. Steam rose from cauldrons. A fat woman with bare and flabby forearms wielded a wooden spoon. Directly in front of the windows and half-obscuring them was a platform from which one could go straight into the main hall of the restaurant. This platform was the stage, and in front of it sat the musicians, a troupe of six men, said to be the six sons of the great Mendel from Berdiczev, whom the oldest Eastern Jews can still remember and whose violin playing was so beautiful that no one who heard it—in Lithuania, Volhynia, or Galicia—ever forgot it.

The actors who were about to appear went by the name of the Surokin Troupe. Surokin was their director, producer, and treasurer, a fat, clean-shaven man from Kovno* who had sung as far afield as America; a cantor and tenor; star of synagogue and opera, pampered, proud, and condescending; in equal parts entrepreneur and comrade. The audience sat at small tables, eating bread and sausages and drinking beer. They went to the kitchen to fetch food and drink, enjoyed themselves, howled and laughed. They were made up of small merchants and their families, not Orthodox but "enlightened," as those Jews are called in the East who shave (even if only once a week) and wear European clothes. Those Jews observe the religious customs more out of pious habit than religious need; they think of God only when they need him, and, given their luck, they need him fairly frequently. They range from the cynical to the superstitious, but in certain situations all of them are apt to be maudlin and touching in their emotionalism. Where business is concerned they will deal with one another and with strangers with complete ruthlessness—but one needs only to touch a certain hidden chord within them and they will be selfless, generous, and humane. Yes, they are perfectly capable of shedding tears, especially in an open-air theater like this one.

The troupe consisted of two women and three men— but when it comes to their performance, I hardly know what to say. The entire program was improvised. First to appear was a small, skinny fellow. The nose in his face

*Now Kaunas, in Lithuania.

looked somehow surprised to be where it was; it was an impertinent, somewhat inquisitive, but still touching and laughable nose, more Slavic than Jewish, broad and flat, coming to an incongruously sharp point. The man with this nose was playing the *batlan*, a wise fool and a jester. He sang old songs and made fun of them by giving them unexpected and unsuitable twists. Then the two women sang an old song together, an actor told a funny story of Shalom Aleichem's, and at the end, Herr Surokin, the director, recited Hebrew and Yiddish poems by recent or contemporary Jewish poets; he would recite the Hebrew verses followed by the Yiddish translation, and sometimes he would sing two or three stanzas as though he were alone in his room. And then there was a deathly hush, and the little merchants made big eyes and propped their chins on their fists, and we could hear the rustling of the linden leaves.

You are probably all familiar with Jewish melodies from the East, but I want to try to give you a sense of that music. I think I can best describe it as a mixture of Russia and Jerusalem, of popular song and psalm. It is music that blends the pathos of the synagogue with the naïveté of folk song. The words, when you read them, would seem to demand a light and jaunty melody. But when you hear the song, it's a sad tune, "smiling through tears." Once having heard it, you remember it weeks later; the contradiction was more apparent than real: In fact these words can *only* be sung to this melody. They go:

Ynter die griene Beimelach
sizzen die Mojschelach, Schlojmelach,
Eugen wie gliehende Keulelach . . .

[Under the green trees
sit the little Solomons and Moseses,
eyes like glowing coalses . . .]

Note, they're sitting! They don't romp about under the green trees. If they were romping, then the rhythm of the line would be as jaunty as it first appears. But then, little Jewish boys don't go in for romping much.

I heard the old song sung by the city of Jerusalem, so melancholy that the pain of it blows right across Europe far into the East, through Spain, Germany, France, Holland—the whole bitter route taken by the Jews. Jerusalem sings:

Kim, kim Jisruleki l aheim
in dein teures Land arain . . .

[Come, come, Jerusalemer, come home
to your beloved homeland . . .]

All the merchants understood it. The little people had stopped drinking beer and eating sausages. In this way they were prepared for the fine, serious, occasionally difficult, and sometimes abstract poetry of the great Hebrew poet Bialik,* whose songs have been translated into most major languages. They are said to have given a new impetus to the transformation of written Hebrew into a living language. This poet has the wrath of the old prophets and the sweetness of the crowing child.

*Hayyim Bialik (1873–1934).

PARIS

I.

It wasn't easy for Eastern Jews to make their way to Paris. Brussels and Amsterdam were both far more obvious destinations. The Jewish gem trade goes to Amsterdam. A few reduced and a few aspiring Jewish gem dealers found themselves compelled to remain on French-speaking territory.

The little Eastern Jew has a somewhat exaggerated fear of a *completely* foreign language. German is almost a mother tongue to him: He would far rather go to Germany than France. The Eastern Jew has a wonderful ear for foreign languages, but his pronunciation is never perfect. It is always possible to pick him out. It's a sound instinct on his part that warns him against the Romance languages.

But even sound instincts may be mistaken. Eastern Jews live almost as well in Paris as God in France.* No one prevents them from having their own businesses, and there are even whole ghettoes here. There are several Jewish quarters in Paris, around Montmartre and close to the Bastille. They are some of the oldest parts of Paris. They are some of the oldest buildings in Paris, with some of the lowest rents. Unless they are very rich, Jews do not like spending their money on "pointless" luxuries.

There are some quite superficial reasons why it should be easier for them in Paris. Their faces do not give them away. Their vivacity does not attract notice. Their sense of humor meets that of the French part way. Paris is a real metropolis. Vienna used to be one. Berlin will one day become one. A real metropolis is objective. Of course it has its prejudices too, but no time to indulge them. In the Vienna Prater there is almost no hint of anti-Semitism, in spite of the fact that not all the visitors are fond of Jews, and they find themselves cheek by jowl with some of the most Eastern of Eastern Jews. And why not? Because people enjoy themselves in the Prater. In the Taborstrasse, on the way back from the Prater, the anti-Semite begins to feel anti-Semitic again. There's no fun to be had on the Taborstrasse.

There's no fun in Berlin. But fun rules in Paris. In Paris

*A play on the German proverb *wie Gott in Frankreich*, meaning "to live well" or "off the fat of the land."

crude anti-Semitism is confined to the joyless, to the royalists, the group around the *Action française*. I am not surprised that the royalists are without influence in France,
and will remain so. They are not French enough. They have
too much pathos and not enough irony.

Paris is objective, though objectivity may be a German virtue. Paris is democratic. The German perhaps has
warmth. But in Paris there is a great tradition of practical
humanity. Paris is where the Eastern Jew begins to become
a Western European. He becomes French. He may even
come to be a French patriot.

2.

The Eastern Jews' bitter existential struggle against
"papers" is less intense in Paris. The police are benignly
remiss. They are more responsive to the individual case
and to personal circumstances. The German police tend
to think in terms of categories. The Parisian policeman is
open to persuasion. It is possible to register in Paris without first experiencing three or four rebuffs.

Eastern Jews are allowed to live as they please in Paris.
They may send their children to Jewish schools or French.
The Paris-born children of Eastern Jews may acquire
French citizenship. France needs inhabitants. It seems to
be positively its duty to be underpopulated, and forever
to stand in need of new inhabitants, and to make foreign-

ers into Frenchmen. In that lies both its strength and its weakness.

Admittedly there is anti-Semitism in France, even outside royalist circles. But it is not one hundred proof. Eastern Jews, accustomed to a far stronger, cruder, more brutal anti-Semitism, are perfectly happy with the French version of it.

And why not? They enjoy religious, cultural, and national rights. They are allowed to speak Yiddish as loudly and as much as they like. They are even allowed to speak bad French without incurring hostility. The consequence of such leniency is that they learn French, and that their children no longer speak Yiddish. At most they still understand it. In the streets of the Jewish quarter of Paris, I was amused to hear the parents speaking Yiddish, and the children replying in French—French answers to Yiddish questions. The children are gifted. They will make something of themselves in France, if God wills. And it seems to me, he does.

The Jewish bars in the Hirtenstrasse in Berlin are sad, cool, and quiet. Jewish establishments in Paris are merry, warm, and noisy. They all do a thriving business. I sometimes eat at Monsieur Weingrod's. He does an excellent roast goose. He distills a good, strong schnapps. He entertains his customers. He says to his wife: "Get me the account book, *s'il vous plaît*." And his wife says: "It's on the table, *si vous voulez*!" They speak a truly wonderful melange.

I asked Monsieur Weingrod: "How did you come to be in Paris?" And Monsieur Weingrod replied: "*Excusez, Monsieur,* why not to Paris? In Russia they throw me out, in Poland they lock me up, in Germany they give me no visa. Why should I not come to Paris, *hein?*"

Monsieur Weingrod is a brave man, he's lost a leg, he has an artificial limb, and he's always in a good mood. He volunteered to fight for France. Many Eastern Jews served in the French army out of gratitude. But Monsieur Weingrod didn't lose his leg in the War. He came home in one piece. But witness the role of fate: Weingrod leaves his restaurant and crosses the street. A car drives down the street perhaps as often as once a week. It chose the precise moment when Monsieur Weingrod was crossing. It ran him over. He lost a leg.

3.

In Paris I visited the Yiddish Theater. Strollers were left in the cloakroom. Umbrellas were taken into the theater. The stalls were full of mothers and infants. The seats were not set in rows; they could be moved around. People wandered up and down the side aisles. One person left his seat, someone else sat down in it. People ate oranges, which squirted aromatically. They spoke aloud, sang along, applauded in midscene. The young Jewish women spoke only French. They were as elegant as Parisiennes. They were beautiful. One might have taken them for women from Marseilles. They have Parisian gifts. They are cool and flirtatious. They are gay and matter-of-fact. They are as faithful as Parisian women. The assimilation of a people always begins with the women. The play was a comedy in three acts. In the first act the Jewish family in a small Russian village wants to emigrate. In the second they get their passports. In the third, the family is in America and has become rich and vulgar. They are in the process of forgetting their former home and their old friends, who have followed them to America. The play offers plenty of opportunities for singing American hit songs and old Russian-Yiddish songs. When the Russian songs and dances were put on, the actors and the audience wept. If it had been just the actors, it would have been kitschy. But when the audience cried too, it was genuinely sad. Jews are easily moved—I knew that. But I didn't know they could be moved by homesickness.

The relationship between stage and audience was close, almost intimate. For Jews it is a fine thing to be an actor. The director came out and announced the next production. Personally—not in the press, not by posters. He said: "Next Wednesday, you will see Monsieur X. from America." He spoke like a leader to his followers. He spoke plainly and wittily. They understood his jokes. Almost got them in advance. Sniffed the punch line.

4.

In France I was talking to a Jewish artiste from the old Russian–Austrian border town of Radziwillow.* He was a musical clown, and he was very successful. He was a clown by conviction, rather than by birth. He came from a family of musicians. His great-grandfather, grandfather, father, and brothers had all been Jewish wedding musicians. He was the only one who had been able to go and study in the West. A wealthy Jew supported him. He was accepted at a conservatory in Vienna. He began to compose his own music. He gave concerts. "But," he said, "what business has a Jew got to be making serious music for the public? I've always been a clown in this world, even if they give lectures on me and a bespectacled newspaper critic sits in the front row. Should I play Beethoven? Should I play *Kol Nidre*?† One evening, as I was standing up on stage, I burst out laughing. A musician from Radziwillow—whom was I trying to fool? Should I go back to Radziwillow and play at Jewish weddings? Or would I make myself even more ridiculous if I did that?

"That evening, it dawned on me that there was nothing else open to me except joining a circus, though not to

*Radziejow.
†Ashkenazi melody for the Day of Atonement, popularized by Max Bruch's cello variations of 1880.

be a bareback rider or an acrobat! That's not for Jews. I'm
a clown. And from my very first appearance in the circus,
I've been utterly convinced that I haven't broken with the
tradition of my forefathers at all, but that what I am is what
they should have been. Admittedly, seeing me would have
come as a shock to them. I play the concertina and the
harmonica and the saxophone, and I'm hugely relieved
that people don't know I can play Beethoven.

"I'm a Yid from Radziwillow.

"I like it in France. Maybe the world is the same all
over for artistes, but not for me. In every city I look for
Jews from Radziwillow. In every city I meet two or three.
We get to talking. There are a few in Paris, too. And if
they're not from Radziwillow, they're from Dubno. And
if they're not from Dubno, then they're from Kishinev.
And they're doing well in Paris. They're really doing well.
Surely not all Jews can belong to the circus? But unless
they're with the circus, they have to suck up to all sorts of
people they don't know and don't like. They can't afford
to be on bad terms with anyone. I just need to be a member of the Performers League. That's a big plus. In Paris,
Jews live at liberty. I'm a patriot; I have a Jewish heart."

5.

Every year a few Jews from the East arrive in the great
port city of Marseilles. They've come to board a ship. Or

they've just disembarked. They were on their way some-where else and ran out of money. They were forced ashore. They drag all their luggage to the post office, while they dictate a telegram and wait for a reply. But telegrams don't always get answered promptly, least of all those that ask for money. Entire families sleep in the open.

A few, a very few, stay in Marseilles. They become interpreters. Interpreting is a Jewish calling. It has nothing to do with translating, say, from English into French, from Russian into French, from German into French. It has to do with translating the stranger, even if he hasn't said anything. He doesn't have to open his mouth. Christian interpreters might translate. Jewish ones intuit.

They earn money. They take strangers into good restaurants and out into the villages too. The interpreters take a cut of the profit. They earn money. They go down to the harbor, they get on a ship, and they go to South America. The United States is difficult for Jews to get into. The quotas were usually exceeded long ago.

6.

A few Eastern Jewish students go to Italy. The Italian government—which has something to atone for—awards scholarships to Jewish students.

Following the collapse of the Dual Monarchy, many

Eastern Jews moved to the newly created South Slav Republic.*

Hungary evicts all Eastern Jews on principle. No Hungarian Jew will take them in. The majority of Hungarian Jews—in spite of Horthy†—are Magyar nationalists. There are rabbis who are Hungarian nationalists.

7.

Where else is there for Eastern Jews to go?

They will not go to Spain. The rabbis placed a solemn curse on Spain when the Jews were forced to leave it. Even nonreligious, "enlightened" Jews are wary of going to Spain. The curse, it so happens, expires this year.

I heard from some Eastern Jewish students that they wanted to go to Spain. They will do well to leave the universities of Poland, where they impose quotas; the University of Vienna, where they impose quotas and bigotry; and the universities of Germany, where they impose the beer stein.

*The later—former—Yugoslavia.
†Admiral Horthy, conservative leader who came to power in Hungary after World War One and ruled until 1944.

8.

It will take a few years yet. Then Eastern Jews will reach Spain. Old legends are told in the East, touching on the long history of the Jews in Spain. There sometimes appears to be a quiet yearning, a suppressed homesickness for this country, which evokes such powerful memories of the original homeland of Palestine.

That said, it's hard to think of any stronger contrast than that between Eastern and Sephardic Jews. Sephardic Jews despise the Ashkenazim in general, and Eastern Jews in particular. The Sephardic Jews are proud of their noble old lineage. Intermarriage between Sephardic and Ashkenazic Jews is extremely rare; between Sephardic and Eastern Jews, almost unheard of.

9.

Once upon a time two Eastern Jews set out on their travels to collect money for the building of a synagogue. They crossed Germany on foot, reached the Rhine, crossed into France, and visited the old Jewish community there, in Montpellier. From there they went east, without a map, without knowing the roads, and got badly lost. One dark night, they found themselves in the perilous country of Spain, where they would certainly have been killed if some devout monks had not taken them in. The monks challenged the Jewish travelers to a theological dispute, were delighted with their erudition, and escorted them safely back across the border. They gave them a lump of gold toward the building of the synagogue. As they said good-bye, the Jews had to promise that they would use the gold for the construction.

The Jews duly promised. Custom (if not the letter of the law) forbade them to use the gold given them by a monastery—even such a friendly one—for their sacred building. For a long time they considered what to do, finally deciding to shape the lump of gold into a ball and fix it on the roof of the synagogue as a kind of emblem.

This golden ball still glitters on the roof of the synagogue. It is the only thing that still connects the Eastern Jews with their erstwhile homeland in Spain.

I heard this story from an old Jew. He was a Torah scribe by profession, a *zophar*, a poor, wise, and deeply religious man. He was opposed to the Zionists.

"Now," he said, "the *cherem*—the anathema, or curse—on Spain will lapse. I have no objection to my grandchildren going to Spain. Jews did not always fare badly there. There were religious people in Spain, and wherever there are devout Christians is a place where Jews can live as well. Because the fear of God is still more dependable than so-called modern humanism."

He didn't know, the old fellow, that humanism is no longer modern. What did he know? he was just a poor Torah scribe.

A Jew Emigrates to America

I.

Even now, and even though the quotas for immigrants from Eastern Europe have been regularly exceeded, and even though American consulates want to see more papers than any consulate on earth, even now, many Eastern Jews emigrate to America.

America signifies distance. America signifies freedom. There is always some relative or other living in America.

It is rare to find a Jewish family in the East that doesn't have an uncle or cousin in America. Somebody emigrated, twenty years ago, say. He fled the draft. Or he received his call-up papers and deserted.

If Eastern Jews weren't quite so timorous, they could take justifiable pride in being the most antimilitaristic people in the world. For a long time they were held by their fatherlands, Russia or Austria, to be unworthy of doing military service. Only when the Jews were accorded equal rights did they have to enlist. It was less a matter of equal rights than equal obligations. Up to that point only the civilian authorities had harrassed the Jews, but now they were exposed to the malignity of the military authorities as well. The Jews bore the slur of not having to fight with great joy. When they were accorded the signal honor of being permitted to fight, drill, and lay down their lives, they were plunged into gloom. Anyone who was approaching his twentieth year and was sufficiently able-bodied to assume that he would be called up fled to America. Whoever could not afford it, mutilated himself. There was a regular epidemic of self-mutilation among Jews in the decades leading up to the War. Their fear of military life induced them to hack off a finger, sever the tendons in their feet, pour corrosives into their eyes. They became heroic cripples, blind, halt, hunchbacked, they subjected themselves to the most lasting and painful disfigurements. They did not want to serve. They did not want to go to war and lose their lives. Their brains were always alert and calculating. Their brains worked out that it is better to live as a cripple than to leave a healthy corpse. Their faith supported their logic. Not only was it stupid to die on behalf of some kaiser or czar or other, it was also a sin to live far from the Torah and in opposition to its teachings. It was a sin to eat pig meat. To bear arms on the Sabbath. To drill. To raise a hand, never mind a sword, against a stranger who has done them no harm. The Eastern Jews were the most heroic of pacifists. They were martyrs for pacifism. They chose crippledom. No one has yet celebrated the heroism of these Jews.

"The commission's on its way!" ran the terror-filled refrain. It referred to the commission of medical examiners that traveled around the shtetls to conscript soldiers. Weeks before, the "torments" had begun. The young Jews tormented themselves to become weak, to cultivate some cardiac irregularity. They didn't sleep, they smoked, they walked, they ran, they were licentious in the service of piety.

Just in case they bribed the army surgeons as well. The chosen middlemen were officials and former army surgeons who had had to quit the service over some shenanigans. Entire tribes of military doctors grew rich, left the army, and went into private practice, part of which consisted in the passing on of bribes.

If you had money you thought about whether you would try bribery or emigrate to America. The courageous ones went to America. They would never come back. They renounced. With a heavy heart they renounced family and with a joyful heart the fatherland.

They went to America.

2.

Today these are the fabled cousins of the Eastern Jews. The onetime deserters have become rich, or at least well-to-do, in the new country. The old Jewish God was with them. He rewarded them for their antimilitarism.

The American cousin is the last hope of every Eastern Jewish family. It's a long time since he last wrote, this cousin. All that's known of him for certain is that he's married and has children. There's an ancient faded photograph of him on the wall. It's been there for the best part of twenty years. It arrived with a ten-dollar bill. Then nothing for the longest time. Even so, the family, back in Dubno, are in no doubt that they'll be able to find him in New York or in Chicago. Of course his name will have become less Jewish, he'll speak English, be an American citizen, wear comfortable suits with baggy pants and padded shoulders. But all the same they will manage to recognize him. Their visit may well be disagreeable to him. But he certainly won't throw them out, for they're kin.

And then one day, while they're thinking about him in these terms, the postman will come with a fat registered letter. The letter will contain dollars, questions, wishes, and greetings, and it will promise: "Steamer ticket to follow."

From that moment on they're "going to America." The seasons change, the months relieve one another, a year elapses, there's nothing more about any steamship ticket, but they're "going to America." The whole shtetl knows it, the surrounding villages know it, the neighboring shtetls know it.

A stranger comes along and asks: "What's Yitzhak Meyer doing?" "He's going to America," the locals will reply; all the while, yesterday and today and tomorrow and the next day, Yitzhak Meyer will be going about his business, and nothing in his home will be any different.

In reality, though, a great deal will be different. He is getting ready. He is getting ready for America. Already he knows exactly what he will take with him and keep, and what he will leave behind and sell. He knows what he wants to do with the quarter of a house that is registered in his name. He inherited a quarter of a house once. The other three-quarters of it belonged to three relations. They've since died or emigrated. Now the other three-quarters belong to a stranger. He could sell him the last remaining quarter, but he wouldn't get much for it. Who else in the world would buy a quarter of a house? So, if it's unmortgaged, he will try and borrow as much as he can on it. After a while he succeeds. He has cash or bills of exchange that are almost as good as cash.

The Jew who intends to go to America doesn't start learning English, as you might have supposed. He already knows how he's going to get along in the new country. He speaks Yiddish, the most widely used language in the world—in terms of geography, not the number of those who speak it. He will make himself understood. He doesn't need to understand English. There are Jews who have lived in the Jewish quarter of New York for thirty years, and they still speak Yiddish and can't understand their own grandchildren.

So he already knows the language of the other country. It is his own mother tongue. And he has money. All he needs now is courage.

It's not America that frightens him, it's the ocean. He

is well used to crossing large expanses of land, but never water. Once, when his forefathers were given a sea to cross, a miracle happened, and the waves parted. If an ocean separates him from his homeland, it's like an eternity. The Eastern Jew is afraid of ships. He doesn't trust them. For centuries he has been living in the interior. The steppes, the limitlessness of the flat land, these hold no terrors for him. What frightens him is disorientation. He is accustomed to turning three times a day toward *Misrach*, the East. It is more than a religious imperative. It is the deeply felt need to know where he is. To know his location. It is easiest to find one's way and to know God's way from the certainty of a geographical location. He knows more or less which way Palestine lies.

At sea, though, he doesn't know where God lives. He can't tell where *Misrach* is. He doesn't know his whereabouts in the world. He isn't free—where he is depends on the course of the ship. Anyone like the Eastern Jew, who, deep within his blood has the knowledge that he might have to flee at any moment, cannot possibly feel at ease on a ship. Where can he run to, if something happens? He's been on the run for thousands of years. For thousands of years menacing things have been happening to him and around him. He has been fleeing for thousands of years. What is he afraid of? Who can tell? Might there not be a pogrom on a ship? Then what?

If a passenger happens to die on board ship, where do they bury the dead man? The corpse is lowered into the water. The old legend of the coming of the Messiah gives a detailed description of the resurrection of the dead. All Jews who are buried in foreign soil will have to roll underground until they reach Palestine. Fortunate are those who are buried there: They are spared the long and laborious journey, the ceaseless rolling for mile upon mile. But will the dead awaken if they have been submerged in the water? Is there land under the water? What strange creatures live down there? A Jew's body may not be cut into pieces. It must be returned to dust whole and unimpaired. But don't sharks devour bodies committed to the water?

In any case the promised steamer ticket hasn't arrived. Of course it's on its way. But it's not sufficient on its own. An entry permit is needed too, and you don't get that without papers. Where are the papers?

And now begins the last, the ultimate, battle for papers, against papers. If the struggle is successful, nothing more is needed. Once in America everyone is automatically issued with a new name and new papers.

Don't be surprised at the Jews' lack of attachment to their names. They will change their names with alacrity, and the names of their fathers, even though those particular sounds, to the European sensibility, are charged with emotional weight.

For Jews their names have no value because they are not their names. Jews, Eastern Jews, have no names. They have compulsory aliases. Their true name is the one by which they are summoned to the Torah on the Sabbath and on holy days: their Jewish first name, and the Jewish first name of their father. Their family names, however, from Goldenberg to Hescheles, are pseudonyms foisted upon them. Governments have commanded Jews to have names. Does that make the names their own? If a man's name is Nachman, and he changes it to the European Norbert, what else is Norbert but camouflage? Is it anything more than a falsification? Does the chameleon feel any respect for the colors he continually keeps changing? In America, the Jew changes Grünbaum to Greenboom. The shift in the vowels doesn't upset him.

3.

Unfortunately, though, he is still not in a position to call himself what he likes. He is still in Poland or in Lithuania. He still needs papers to confirm his birth, his existence, his identity.

And he begins to walk the paths that, in their small, microcosmic way, are just as tangled, as unpredictable, as ridiculous, and as tragic as those his fathers walked before him. He doesn't get sent from Pontius to Pilate,* but more like from the anteroom of Pontius to the locked door of Pilate. All official doors are barred to him. It takes a petty

---

*The equivalent, and possibly the origin, of the English expression "from pillar to post."

bureaucrat to unlock them. But if anyone takes sadistic pleasure in turning people away, then it's petty bureaucrats.

Can they be bribed? As if that were straightforward! Can you be sure that an attempt at bribery wouldn't involve you in some huge court case where you wind up in prison? The only thing that may be said with confidence is that all officials are corruptible. Yes, everyone is corruptible. Corruptibility is a prime human virtue. But if and when someone will admit his corruptibility remains a great imponderable. It is not impossible that an official, having taken money on ten previous occasions, will bring charges against you on the eleventh, to prove his innocence on those ten occasions and to allow him another hundred with impunity.

Luckily there are people almost everywhere with precise insight into the official's soul. They live from their knowledge. Moreover these experts are Jews. But because they are so rarely met with in every town, and because they have the ability to drink with the officials in the local language, these Jews are practically officials themselves, and you need to bribe them before you can even think of the actual bribing.

But even a successfully completed bribe saves you no humiliation and no wasted journeys. You suffer the humiliations and you embark on the wasted journeys.

And then you have your papers.

4.

And then when everything has been done, America shuts down its borders again, says it's had enough Eastern Jews for another year, and so you sit down and you wait till next year.

Then at last you travel by fourth-class rail to Hamburg. It takes six days. You spend another two weeks waiting for the ship. Finally you embark. And while all the other passengers are waving their handkerchiefs, close to tears, the Jewish emigrant for the first time in his life rejoices. He is afraid, but he trusts in his God. He is on his way to a country that greets all new arrivals with a gigantic statue of liberty. The reality must somehow correspond to this enormous monument.

To some extent, the reality *does* correspond to the symbol. Not because they really are all that serious about liberty in the new country, but because they have people who are more Jewish than the Jews, which is to say the Negroes. Of course Jews are still Jews. But here, significantly, they are first and foremost whites. For the first time a Jew's race is actually to his advantage.

The Eastern Jew travels third class or in steerage. The crossing is easier than he imagined, but getting ashore is much harder.

The medical examination in the European port was bad enough. Now there is a still-more-rigorous one. And something turns out to be not quite right with your papers.

The papers are genuine, and very hard to obtain too, but they still look somehow not quite right.

Possible too that some vermin has got into the Jew's shirt during the crossing.

Everything is possible.

And so the Jew winds up in a kind of prison that goes by the name of "quarantine," or somesuch.

A high fence protects America from him.

Through the bars of his prison, he sees the Statue of Liberty, and he doesn't know whether it's himself or Liberty that has been incarcerated.

He thinks about what New York will be like. He can hardly imagine it.

It will be this way: He will live among twelve-story buildings, surrounded by Chinese, Hungarians, and other Jews. Once more he will be a peddler, once more fear the police, once more be bullied.

His children will perhaps become Americans. Perhaps rich and famous Americans. Kings of some mineral or manufactured substance.

These are the dreams of the Jew, behind bars in his quarantine.

THE CONDITION OF THE JEWS IN SOVIET RUSSIA

he Jews were a recognized "national minority" in czarist Russia, but they were persecuted. Contempt, oppression, and pogroms confirmed the status of the Jews. There were no efforts to assimilate them by, say, programmatic rapes. The effort was to exclude them. The means employed looked more like an attempt to eradicate them.

In Western Europe, anti-Semitism was a private reflex. In the Christian Middle Ages, it was a facet of religious fanaticism. In Russia anti-Semitism was a pillar of government. The simple peasant, the *muzhik*, was not anti-Semitic. The Jew was not a friend to him, but a stranger. Russia, which had so much room for strangers, was also open to them. In contrast, it was the half-educated and the middle classes who were anti-Semites, who became so because the nobility was. The nobility was because the court was. The court was because the czar, for whom it was not acceptable to fear his own Orthodox "children,"

could only claim to be afraid of the Jews. Characteristics were therefore ascribed to them that made them appear dangerous to every class: To the simple "man of the people" they were ritual murderers; to the small landowner they were destroyers of property; to the senior official they were common swindlers; to the nobility, clever—and therefore dangerous—serfs; and finally, to the bureaucrat, the quintessential petty official, they were ritual murderers, hucksters, revolutionaries, and plebeians—everything rolled into one.

The eighteenth century brought with it the emancipation of the Jews in Western countries. State-legitimized anti-Semitism only began in the next century in Russia. Plehve, later to be minister,* organized the first pogroms in southern Russia in 1881–82. They were intended to intimidate young Jewish revolutionaries. But the hired crowds, less interested in the avenging of past acts of terror than in the collecting of booty, ransacked the houses of wealthy conservative Jews, who were not the intended victims at all. There was, therefore, a switch in policy to the so-called "silent pogrom," to the creation of "settlement zones," to the eviction of Jewish artisans from the big cities. Quotas were set for Jewish schools (three per one hundred), and oppressive measures were initiated against Jewish intelligentsia in the universities. But realizing that the Jewish railway millionaire Poliakov was a close per-

---

*Vyacheslav Plehve (1846–1904), czarist minister of the interior.

sonal friend of the czar and that his employees were permitted to remain in the big cities, thousands of Russian Jews became "employees" of Poliakov. There were many such dodges. The resourcefulness of the Jews was met halfway by the corruptibility of the officials. Only in the early years of the twentieth century was there a return to the open pogroms and the ritual murder trials. . . .

Today Soviet Russia is the only country in Europe where anti-Semitism is scorned, though it might not have ceased. Jews are entirely free citizens—though their freedom may not yet signify that a solution of the Jewish question is at hand. As individuals they are free from hatred and persecution. As a people they have *all* the rights of a "national minority." In the history of the Jews, such a sudden and complete liberation is unexampled.

Of the 2.75 million Jews in Russia, there are 300,000 organized workers and employees; 130,000 peasants; 700,000 artisans and self-employed. The remainder consists of (*a*) capitalists and "déclassé" individuals, who are described as "unproductive elements"; (*b*) small traders, middlemen, agents, and hawkers, who are seen as unproductive but proletarian individuals. The *colonization* of Jews is going on apace—partly with American funds, which before the Revolution all went into the colonization of Palestine. There are Jewish colonies in the Ukraine, near Odessa; and in the Crimea, near Kherson. Since the Revolution, some 6,000 Jewish families have been taken into agricultural labor. All in all 102,000 dessiatines* of land have been distributed among Jewish farmers. Simultaneously the Jews are being "industrialized"—in other words, there is an effort to bring in "unproductive elements" as factory workers and to train young people as specialist workers in some thirty professional-technical schools reserved for Jews.

Wherever there are large Jewish populations, there are schools with Yiddish as the principal language. In the Ukraine alone, some 350,000 attend such schools; in Byelorussia,† the figure is in the vicinity of 90,000. In the Ukraine, thirty-three courts conduct their hearings in Yiddish. There are Jewish presidents of district courts and Jewish militia (police) units. There are three major Yiddish newspapers, three weeklies, five monthlies, several Jewish state theaters, and a high proportion of Jewish students in the universities and in the Communist Party. There are some 600,000 Jewish Young Communists.

This handful of facts and figures will show how the Soviet Union is tackling the Jewish question: with unshakable belief in the infallibility of theory, with a somewhat naive and undifferentiated but pure and austere idealism. What does theory call for?—national self-determination! But in order to apply the prescription in full, the Jews first need to be made into a "legitimate" national minority, like

---

*A dessiatine is a Russian unit of land measure equal to 2.7 acres.
†Now Belarus.

the Grusinians, or the Germans, or the Byelorussians. The unnatural social structure of the Jews must be transformed, for this is a people that—of all the peoples in the world—has the most beggars; the most "welfare recipients," as the Americans say; the most downwardly mobile. They must be molded into a people with familiar and reliable characteristics. And because this new nationality is to live in a socialist state, its "unproductive" and lower-middle-class elements must be converted into workers and peasants. And finally they will be rewarded by their very own piece of territory somewhere.

Obviously one can't expect such a bold attempt to succeed overnight. The misery of the Jewish poor is only slightly alleviated by their new freedoms. However many choose to emigrate to new territories, the old ghettoes remain overcrowded. I suspect that the Jewish proletarian is worse off than any other. I had my most depressing experience during a tour of the Jewish quarter of Odessa, known as the Moldovanka. The evening there is a curse, the rising moon a mockery. A thick fog presses down like a condemnation. Beggars are not merely the public face of the town, they are beggars three times over, because they are the residents. Every house comprises five, six, or seven tiny stores. Every store doubles as an apartment. Behind each window, which also serves as a door, is the workshop; behind that is the bed. Over the bed are the children, suspended in bassinets, which misery rocks to and fro. Large, burly men come home: They are Jewish dockworkers from the port. They look strange, surrounded by their small, weak, pale, and hysterical fellow countrymen—a wild, barbarian race in the middle of old Semites. All the workers labor until late at night. The windows leak a drab yellow light. A strange light that doesn't spread brightness but a kind of gloom with a pale kernel. Unrelated to any sacred flame. The soul of darkness . . .

The old questions, the crucial questions, aren't even addressed by the Revolution: Are the Jews a nation like any other, or are they more or less; are they a religious community, a tribal community, or do they merely share certain intellectual features? And is it possible to regard a people that has preserved itself in Europe purely by its religion and its historical separation as a "people," and leave religion out of it? Is it possible to make a separation between church and nationality in this case; is it possible to make peasants out of people with inherited intellectual attributes, or specimens of mass psychology out of a race of strongly marked individuals?

I have seen many Jewish peasants. They have truly lost all their ghetto traits. They are rustic types, but they are easily distinguished from other peasants. The Russian peasant is a peasant first and a Russian second; the Jew is Jew first and then peasant. I know that this formulation will provoke every hardheaded reader to say: "Who told you?!"

But I have seen it. I have seen that four thousand years of being a Jew, nothing but a Jew, have not been without effect. It's an old destiny, an old, richly experienced blood. Jews are of an intellectual cast. They are a people that has had no illiterates for nearly two thousand years now; a people with more periodicals than newspapers; a people whose periodicals, probably uniquely in the world, have a far higher readership than its newspapers. While the other peasants around him are finally struggling to read and write, the Jew, behind his plow has his mind on the problems of relativity theory. No machinery has been invented for peasants with such an advanced brain. Primitive gear demands a primitive mind. Even a tractor is a simple tool, compared to the dialectical intelligence of the Jew. The new Jewish colonies may be well kept, clean, and profitable. (To date there are also very few of them.) But they remain "colonies," they have not become villages.

I can see the obvious objection: The awl, the plane, the hammer of the Jewish artisan are certainly no more sophisticated than the plow. But the work is also more directly creative. In the making of a loaf of bread, most of the work is done by nature. In the making of a boot, it is done by man.

I can see a second objection, too: that so many Jews work in factories. But in the first place, most of them are trained specialists; second, they manage to divert their hungry minds from purely mechanical labor by intellectual hobbies, by artistic dilettantism, by political activism, avid reading, or writing for newspapers; and third, one may observe, if not a stream, then at least a steady trickle of Jews leaving the factories, especially in Russia. They leave to become self-employed craftsmen if not entrepreneurs.

Can, say, a little Jewish "matchmaker" ever be turned into a peasant? His occupation is not only unproductive, it is, by some lights, even immoral. He has lived badly, not earned very much, existed more by scrounging than by working. But what intricate, difficult, albeit reprehensible work his brain has had to do to find a "match," and to extort a substantial tip from a rich, miserly fellow citizen! What will his brain do in the ghastly quiet of his new existence?

The "productivity" of the Jews has never been crassly visible in any case. If twenty generations of unproductive introspectives have lived to produce one Spinoza; if it took ten generations of rabbis and traders to spawn a *single* Mendelssohn; if thirty generations of mendicant wedding musicians have been fiddling away so that *one* famous virtuoso is born; then I for one am not against such "unproductiveness." Maybe we wouldn't have had Marx and Lassalle either, if their forefathers had been turned into peasants.

If synagogues are now being transformed into workmen's clubs in Soviet Russia, and Talmud schools are banned on the grounds that they are religious establishments, then we need to be very sure about the distinctions between knowledge, religion, and nationality with Eastern Jews. But it seems clear to me that knowledge is religion, and religion is—nationality. Their clergy are their men of learning, and their prayer is an expression of nationhood. But the entity that is now set to enjoy the rights and freedoms of a "national minority" in the Soviet Union is a different sort of Jewish nation. They are a people with old heads and new hands, with old blood and a relatively new written language, with old gifts and a new national culture. Zionism wanted to combine tradition with progressive thinking. The Jewish minority in Russia does not look back at all: They don't want to be the *heirs* of the old Hebrews, merely their descendants.

Inevitably the sudden freedom of Russian Jews provokes a vehement, if stifled, anti-Semitism here and there. When an unemployed Russian sees a Jew taken on by a factory in order to become "industrialized," when an expropriated *kulak* gets to hear of more Jewish colonization, then an ugly, old, artificially nurtured instinct is bound to rear its head again. But while anti-Semitism has become a subject for study in the West, and blood lust a political point of view, in the new Russia, it remains a disgrace. What will ultimately kill it off is public shame.

Once the Jewish question is solved in Russia, then it is on the way to being solved everywhere. (There is hardly any Jewish emigration from Russia anymore, if anything net *im*migration.) The piety of the population is declining rapidly. The stronger barriers of religion are falling, replaced by the weaker ones of nationality. If this process continues, the age of Zionism will have passed, along with the age of anti-Semitism—and perhaps even that of Judaism itself. It is a development that will be welcomed in some places and regretted in others. But everyone should take notice as one people is freed from the stain of suffering and another from the stain of cruelty. The victim is freed from his torments and the bully from his compulsion. This is a great accomplishment of the Russian Revolution.

Afterword

I t is my duty to alert the esteemed reader to the fact that the position of the Jews in the Soviet Union, as I tried to describe it in the last section of my book, has in all likelihood changed since that time. No figures or statistics are available to me. Those I cited previously I collected myself on a fact-finding visit to Russia. I cannot give the same credence to the tendentious and unreliable figures I might be able to get from Moscow now. I remain convinced, however, that nothing in the *underlying* attitude of Soviet Russia toward the Jews has altered. It is this underlying truth that matters, not the figures.

At this point I should like to refer to the grimmest development in recent years: I mean of course the Spanish Civil War. A minority of readers will be aware of the version of the story according to which the *cherem*, the rabbinical curse that was laid on Spain following its eviction of the Jews, is presently about to lapse. I am of course not claiming any explicit connection between the meta-physical curse and the grim reality. But I trust I may be permitted to draw the reader's attention to the facts.

I don't want to be misunderstood as saying: Just as the curse is wearing off, Spain is experiencing the greatest catastrophe in its history. I want only to point out the—certainly more than curious—coincidence of timing; and to quote the sentence of the fathers that goes:"The Court of the Lord is in continuous session, here on earth and in the hereafter."

Centuries may pass—but the judgment is ineluctable.

—JOSEPH ROTH
June 1937

PREFACE TO THE NEW EDITION (1937)

I.

Many years ago, when I wrote this book, which I now hope to set before the reader in revised form, there was no acute problem affecting the Jews of Western Europe. What mattered then was to persuade the Jews and non-Jews of Western Europe to grasp the tragedy of the Eastern Jews—and especially in the land of unlimited opportunity, by which of course I mean not America but Germany. There was of course a degree of latent anti-Semitism there (like everywhere else). Most German Jews regarded themselves, despite an abundance of clearly threatening evidence of anti-Semitism, as perfectly good Germans; on High Holy Days, at most, they thought of themselves as Jewish Germans. They took great pains either to take no account of latent anti-Semitism or to overlook it altogether. In the case of many or even most

Western Jews, they attempted to replace the lost or diluted faith of their fathers with a willful blindness, which I describe as a superstitious belief in progress. Some of them unfortunately gave in to the temptation to blame Jewish immigrants from the East for the expression of anti-Semitic feeling. It is an oft-ignored fact that Jews, too, are capable of anti-Semitism. One does not want to be reminded by some recent arrival from Lodz of one's own grandfather from Posen* or Katowice. This is the unworthy but understandable attitude of an insecure middle class just scaling the steep ladder into the echelons of the upper middle class, with fresh air and scenic views. At the sight of a cousin from Lodz, one may easily lose one's balance and fall.

In the attempt to reach that ledge where, under certain circumstances, aristocrats, Christian industrialists, and Jewish financiers were prepared to claim that they were all equal, and emphasized their equality so vociferously that no sensitive ear could fail to grasp that what they were really emphasizing was their inequality, the German Jew tossed his coreligionists the occasional sop, so as not to be hindered in his personal ascent. Giving a sop to strangers is perhaps the meanest form of hospitality, but it is hospitality nonetheless. There were some German Jews—and one of their representatives is today languishing in a concentration camp—who not only imagined that every-

*Now Poznan.

thing would be fine but for the arrival of Jews from the East, but who actually helped sic the plebeian bailiff on the helpless strangers, as one sets a dog on a tramp. But when the bailiff took power, and the janitor took over the "state apartments," and the guard dogs broke free, then the German Jew was forced to see that he was more exposed and more homeless even than his cousin in Lodz had been a few years before. The German Jew had grown arrogant. He had lost the God of his fathers and acquired an idol instead: the idol of a civilizatory patriotism. But God had not forgotten him. And he sent him on his wanderings, a tribulation that is appropriate to Jews, and to all others besides. Lest we forget that nothing in this world endures, not even a home; and that our life is short, shorter even than the life of the elephant, the crocodile, and the crow. Even parrots outlive us.

2.

It seems I must now defend German Jews against their cousins from Lodz, just as I attempted previously to defend the Lodz cousins against attacks by the Germans. In a way the German Jew is even worse off than the Eastern Jew. He has forgotten how to wander, how to suffer, and how to pray. All he knows is how to work—which is what he is not allowed to do. Of the six hundred thousand German Jews, some one hundred thousand or so have emigrated. The majority of those remaining are unable to find work. They are not even allowed to look for it. Their passports expire and become invalid. And a human life nowadays hangs from a passport as it once used to hang by the fabled thread. The scissors once wielded by the Fates have come into the possession of consulates, embassies, and plainclothesmen. No one loves victims, not even their fellow victims. At most they are loved by holy and devout people, who are as despised in this vulgarized world as the Jews are. Where can they go? With his senses sharpened by despair, the emigrant can hear the inaudible call to him from every border: "Die miserably where you are!"

Émigré German Jews are like a new tribe: Having forgotten how to be Jews, they are learning it all over again. They are unable to forget that they are German, and they can't lose their Germanness. They are like snails with two shells on their backs. Abroad, even overseas, they appear German. It's difficult for them to deny, if they are to be truthful. Oh—the whole world thinks in such tired, worn, traditional clichés. It never asks the wanderer where he's going, only ever where he's come from. And what matters to the wanderer is his destination, not his point of departure.

3.

When a catastrophe occurs, people at hand are shocked into helpfulness. Certainly, acute catastrophes have that effect. It seems that people expect catastrophes to be brief. But chronic catastrophes are so unpalatable to neighbors that they gradually become indifferent to them and their victims, if not downright impatient. The sense of order, regularity, and due process is so deeply ingrained in people that they are only willing to entertain the opposite— emergency, madness, chaos, confusion—for a brief period. Once the emergency becomes protracted, helping hands return to pockets, the fires of compassion cool down. People become inured to their own misfortunes, so why not the misfortunes of their neighbors and, in particular, the misfortunes of the Jews?

Plenty of welfare committees have been dissolved, voluntarily or otherwise. A few generous philanthropists are hardly in a position to cope with mass distress. Every European country has stopped taking in so-called "intellectual" émigrés, and so have their colonies. Palestine, as everyone knows, has been able to take in no more than a few thousand. Many return from places like Argentina, Brazil, and Australia after only a short time. The various countries proved unable to keep the promises the committees made on their behalf. I don't know what sort of shape the people are in who are still there: By which I mean I don't know if they're alive or dead. From time to time an individual may get through: That's the law of nature. The world hasn't helped much, not even out of expediency. But then, how could one have looked to a world like this for help?

4.

In such a world, not only is it out of the question that émigrés should be offered bread and work but it is taken for granted. It has also become out of the question for them to be issued so-called papers. And what is a man without papers? Rather less, let me tell you, than papers without a man! The so-called Nansen passport* that Russian émigrés were furnished after the Revolution, and which, incidentally, failed to secure them freedom of movement, is not even a possibility for German émigrés. The League of Nations now has a department—with a British high commissioner in charge of it—which is responsible for regulating the official status of German émigrés. But we know all about the League of Nations—its turgid bureaucracy and the golden shackles that its best-intentioned commissioners wear. The only country that

---

*An identification card for stateless persons, introduced in 1922 by the Norwegian polar explorer and civil rights campaigner Fridtjof Nansen (1861–1930), who was awarded the Nobel Peace Prize that same year.

so far has issued valid papers to German émigrés is France, although these again do not offer proper freedom of movement for those who hold them. Even these papers, however, were only made available to a limited number of émigrés, who had entered France before a certain date—and even then, only under certain conditions. It is difficult, if not impossible, to get even this legal document stamped with the visa of any other country. Italy, Poland, Lithuania, even England, are all reluctant to admit stateless travelers. In effect, only "prominent" refugees are able to travel on them—Jewish journalists, newspaper publishers, film actors, or directors: people who are well acquainted with the ambassadors and consuls. How will a poor Jewish tailor ever get into the visa department of a consulate or an embassy? It's almost a metaphysical affliction: You're a transient and you're stuck; a refugee and a detainee; condemned to rootlessness and unable to budge. And even for such tender mercies, you owe thanks to the Almighty, and in particular, to the police.

In some of the most civilized nations of Europe, the local animal protection societies organize curious airborne expeditions: They collect migrating birds that for one reason or another were left behind by their fellows in the autumn. They put them in cages and fly them to Italy—where they are shot down and eaten by an enthusiastic population. Is there a comparable society for the protection of humans, one prepared to take our fellow beings, those without passports and visas, to the land of their heart's desire? Are five thousand swallows, who stayed behind for some unknown and unknowable natural reason, worth more than fifty thousand human beings? A bird doesn't need a ticket, a passport, a visa—and a human being gets put away because he's short of just one of those items? Do people feel more compassion toward birds than toward other people? Cruelty to animals is punished, yet cruelty to humans brings promotion. Just like migrating birds—though without quite the same imperative—they too are periodically shipped north or south in airplanes. No wonder that animal welfare groups enjoy more popularity in every country, and with every level of the people, than does the League of Nations.

5.

Also condemned to wander are those Jews who have remained in Germany. From their small towns, they are forced to move into large towns, and then cities, and when they are booted out of those, back into smaller towns. But even if they manage to remain technically in one place, what inner wanderings they are put through! They wander away from friends, from familiar greetings, from kind words. They shut their eyes to deny what has just happened, which is to wander into a self-willed illusion of night. They wander away from the shock they have just experienced, into fear, which is the older sister of shock, and try to feel comfortable and at ease with fear. They wander into deception, and the worst kind of deception at that—self-deception. And they also wander from one branch of officialdom to the next, from the local police station to the central police headquarters, from the tax inspectorate to the National Socialist Party offices, from the concentration camp back to the police, and from there to the law court, from the law court to prison, from prison to the house of correction. The child of German Jews embarks on its extraordinary wanderings at a tender age, going from natural trustingness to suspicion, fear, hatred, and alienation. It sidles into the classroom, past the benches from the front to the back, and even if it has a place, it still has the sensation of wandering. The Jew wanders from one Nuremberg Law to the next,* from one newspaper stand to the next, as though in the hope of finding the truth on sale there one day. He wanders toward the dangerous bromide that says: "All things come to an end!" without thinking that he himself is liable to come to an end sooner rather than later. He wanders— staggers, rather—into the fatuous hope: "It won't be as bad as all that!"—and that hope is nothing but moral corruption.

*The Nuremberg Laws were two measures designed by Hitler and approved by the Nazi Party Conference in September 1935. The first stripped Jews of German citizenship, making them "subjects of the state"; the second forbade marriage or sexual relations between Jews and Aryans. They were followed by further enactments.

They stay, and at the same time they wander: It's a kind of contortionism of which only the most desperate prisoners are capable.

It is the prison of the Jews.

6.

It is worse than Babylonish captivity. Not only may the Jews not bathe on the banks of the Spree, the Elbe, the Main, the Rhine, the Danube, neither may they sit down and weep; they are only allowed to do this in the so-called Kulturbund, the officially sanctioned centerpiece of the new ghetto.

This Kulturbund, however high-minded its inception, is nothing more or less than an unwarranted concession on the part of the Jews to the barbarous theories of National Socialism. Its basis is not the assumption—accepted by so many Jews today—that they are a separate race, but the implicit admission that they are an *inferior* one. Whereas no one would have dreamed of forbidding some Tibetan, Caucasian, or Japanese Kulturbund to perform Goethe or Beethoven, the Jewish Kulturbund is not allowed to do so. Even when German Jews agree with the National Socialists that they are a distinct people from the Germans (albeit a "guest people" of theirs for a very long time), it is a grave discrimination when these German Jews cannot put on such art. Yet the Kulturbund Jews have simply accepted this discrimination as a given. They were treated not as a minority but as an *inferiority*. To them it seemed perfectly natural. Their projects, their concerts, their meetings, were supervised by a commissioner, to whom they have to show respect, just as in the dives around Berlin's Alexanderplatz the "widows' dances" were once supervised by police commissioners.

Is it correct to speak of a lack of pride on the part of German Jews? I am apt to feel a little sentimental about them, which precludes true empathy. When the subject is the flaws of German Jews, it is not possible to "turn a blind eye." They might deserve our forbearance but not our blindness. During the pogroms in Kishinev—how much time has passed since Europe was properly Europe, and England told the czar what it today modestly declines to pass on to a former World War One corporal—the Jews fought back. They beat sixty-one Cossacks to death. The Jewish butchers in Hungary opposed the "White" hordes, often putting them to flight. Yet in Germany only a single Jew fired a gun on the day of the "boycott" (and of course, he was put to death).

How does one account for this craven way of responding to so much vileness and treachery? Is it religion? The majority of German Jews paid taxes to the Israelite religious community. Many subscribed to the *Hamburg Israelite Family Sheet*—and that was about the extent of

their commitment to Judaism. (Of course I'm not referring to Zionists and "nationally conscious" Jews here, but
to "German citizens of the Jewish faith.") The names of
their brothers who fell for Germany are erased from mon-
uments and memorials—in a two-pronged attack on the
dead and the living—they are legally deprived of bread,
work, honor, and property, but they button their lips and
carry on. No fewer than five hundred thousand people
continue to live in this humiliated condition, go out on
the peaceful street, take the streetcar and the train, pay their
taxes, and write letters: There is no limit to the amount of
abuse a man is prepared to take, once he has lost his pride.

German Jews are doubly unhappy: They not only suffer humiliation, they endure it. The ability to endure it is
the greater part of their tragedy.

7.

There is no counsel, no consolation, no hope. We
need to be clear about the fact that there is no compro-
mising with racism. Millions of plebeians badly need a
few hundred thousand wretched Jews to confirm their
own superiority. The Hohenzollerns (and with them the
whole of German aristocracy) have already kowtowed to
the janitors. What can a Jew expect? The masses are unap-
peasable enough when they gang up and follow their own

lawless instincts. What will they be like given a measure of organization? If it's any comfort to the German Jews, they might reflect that the Hohenzollerns are in the same boat (though admittedly, that house is of much more recent origins than the Jewish race).

Nothing would have damaged the National Socialist regime as much as the prompt and well-organized departure of all Jews and their descendants from Germany. National Socialism loses its coherence the moment it enters any sort of negotiation with the Jews. Its own aims are far distant, and in a direction that does not directly concern the Jews.

National Socialism may say "Jerusalem," but what it really means is: "Jerusalem and Rome."

8.

Only a very small, select minority of devout Christians have understood that—for the first time in the long and shameful history of Jewish persecution—the plight of the Jews is identical to that of the Christians. They beat up Moritz Finkelstein from Wroclaw, but the intended victim is Jesus of Nazareth. They take away the license of a Jewish livestock dealer from Fürth or Nuremberg, but on their minds is the shepherd in Rome who pastures his devout flock. Clearly it's not enough to defame and torment a few hundred thousand people who share a common origin. The sons of the tide-waiters* demand vengeance for the expulsion of the customs men. That's the real "voice of blood." You can hear it shouting from every loudspeaker.

Admittedly many of the Christian faith—among them, many high Church dignitaries—are impervious to this insight. The goings on in the Third Reich will teach them. In their deludedness, these Christians are almost like German Jews. They will one day understand that the banal witticism applied to the Jews—"You can't baptize it out of them"—really applies to the Third Reich.

Not even by concordats.

9.

In all probability only a small proportion of the Jews still living in Germany today will be able to—and will want to—emigrate. After a century of emancipation, and the semblance of equal rights for the past fifty years, these Jews may not have the divine grace of suffering that their pious brothers do. But they do have an extraordinary capacity to endure indescribable things. So they will stay, they will marry, they will procreate, they will pass on their

---

*A customs inspector who boards ships and monitors the landing of goods.

glooms and their bitternesses—all in the hope that one day "it will all be different."

One day—and well before the thousand years are up—things will indeed be different in Germany. But neither Jews nor Christians nor indeed civilized Europeans will have any joy with the generation currently in the Hitler Youth. They are Jason's brood, sown from dragon's teeth. It will take a whole army of missionaries to baptize the coming generations of German heathens. So long as the Germans are not Christianized, Jews will have little to hope for at their hands.

It therefore seems probable that the Jews will keep their pariah status in German society for many years to come. It seems unduly optimistic to hope that Europe might recover its conscience, that a widely accepted law might overturn the mistaken principle of "noninvolvement," which merely amplifies the vulgar proverb: "You sweep outside your own door." This janitorial philosophy has now governed history for the last few decades. Instead, everyone ought to sweep outside one another's door. It cannot be wrong for me to barge into my neighbor's house if my neighbor is just about to take an ax to his children. There can be no European or European-Christian morality so long as the principle of "noninvolvement" is respected. What is it that allows European states to go spreading civilization and ethics in foreign parts but not at home? Centuries of civilization are no guarantee that a European people, by some ghastly curse of fate, will not revert to barbarism. Even among the peoples of Africa, which today require the protection* of civilized peoples, there must have been some whose millennial civilization one day—or, one century, one might say—was suddenly and inexplicably destroyed. European scholarship tells us as much.

People are forever talking about a "European family of nations." But if there is to be any truth in those words: Have you ever seen a brother fail to restrain his brother's hand when he's about to perpetrate some heinous or idiotic act? Am I really only permitted to teach morality to the black headhunter, and not the white? A chilly sort of family, this "family of nations"! . . . The father is quite set on only sweeping outside his own door, while the stench from his son's room rises to high heaven.

10.

I wish I had the grace and the insight to suggest some way out of our present difficulties. But honesty, one of the often unsung muses of the writer, forces me to bring this second foreword of mine to a pessimistic conclusion:

1. Zionism can bring only a partial solution to the Jewish question.

*An ironic reference to Abyssinia, invaded by Italy.

2. Jews will only attain complete equality, and the dignity of external freedom, once their "host-nations" have attained their own inner freedom, as well as the dignity conferred by sympathy for the plight of others.

3. It is—failing some divine intervention—hardly possible to believe that the "host-nations" will find such freedom and such dignity.

Pious Jews may be left with the consolation of the here-after.

As for the rest, it's "*vae victis.*"

Joseph Roth

CREDITS

ABOUT THE
AUTHOR

Joseph Roth was born Moses Joseph Roth to Jewish parents on September 2, 1894, in Brody in Galicia, in the extreme east of the then Hapsburg Empire; he died on May 27, 1939, in Paris. He never saw his father—who disappeared before he was born and later died insane—but grew up with his mother and her relatives. After completing school in Brody, he matriculated at the University of Lemberg (variously Lvov or Lviv), before transferring to the University of Vienna in 1914. He served for a year or two with the Austro-Hungarian Army on the Eastern Front—though possibly only as an army journalist or censor. Later he was to write: "My strongest experience was the War and the destruction of my fatherland, the only one I ever had, the Dual Monarchy of Austria-Hungary."

In 1918 he returned to Vienna, where he began writing for left-wing papers, occasionally as "Red Roth," "*der rote Roth*." In 1920 he moved to Berlin, and in 1923 he began his distinguished association with the *Frankfurter Zeitung*. In the following years, he traveled throughout Europe, filing copy for the *Frankfurter* from the south of France, the USSR, Albania, Germany, Poland, and Italy. He was one of the most distinguished and best-paid journalists of the period—being paid at the dream rate of one Deutschmark per line. Some of his pieces were collected under the title of one of them, *The Panopticum on Sunday* (1928), while some of his reportage from the Soviet Union went into *The Wandering Jews*. His gifts of style and perception could, on occasion, overwhelm his subjects, but he was a journalist of singular compassion. He observed and warned of the rising Nazi scene in Germany (Hitler actually appears by name in Roth's first novel, in 1923), and his 1926 visit to the USSR disabused him of most—but not quite all—of his sympathy for Communism.

When the Nazis took power in Germany in 1933, Roth immediately severed all his ties with the country. He lived in Paris—where he had been based for some years—but also in Amsterdam, Ostend, and the south of France, and wrote for émigré publications. His royalist politics were mainly a mask for his pessimism; his last article was called "Goethe's Oak at Buchenwald." His final years were difficult; he moved from hotel to hotel, drinking heavily, worried about money and the future. What precipitated his final collapse was hearing the news that the playwright Ernst Toller had hanged himself in New York. An invitation from the American PEN Club (the organization that had brought Thomas Mann and many others to the States) was found among Roth's papers. It is tantalizing but ultimately impossible to imagine him taking ship to the New World, and continuing to live and to write: His world was the old one, and he'd used it all up.

Roth's fiction came into being alongside his journalism, and in the same way: at café tables, at odd hours and all hours, peripatetically, chaotically, charmedly. His first novel, *The Spider's Web*, was published in installments in 1923. There followed *Hotel Savoy* and *Rebellion* (both 1924), hard-hitting books about contemporary society and politics; then *Flight Without End*, *Zipper and His Father*, and *Right and Left* (all *Heimkehrerromane*—novels about soldiers returning home after the war). *Job* (1930) was his first book to draw considerably on his Jewish past in the East. *The Radetzky March* (1932) has the biggest scope of all his books and is commonly reckoned his masterpiece. There follow the books he wrote in exile, books with a stronger fabulist streak in them, full of melancholy beauty: *Tarabas, The Hundred Days, Confession of a Murderer, Weights and Measures, The Emperor's Tomb*, and *The Tale of the 1002nd Night*.

About the
Translator

Michael Hofmann, the son of the German novelist Gert Hofmann, was born in 1957 in Freiburg. At the age of four he moved to England, where he has lived, off and on, ever since. After studying English at Cambridge, and comparative literature by himself, he moved to London in 1983. He has published poems and reviews widely in England and the United States. In 1993 he was appointed Distinguished Lecturer at the English Department of the University of Florida in Gainesville.

To date he has published four books of poems and a collection of criticism, *Farthingale to Astrakhon*, all with Faber & Faber. He edited (with James Lasdun) a book of contemporary versions of the *Metamorphoses*, called *After Ovid*, and is now editing *Rilke in English* for Penguin. He has translated Kafka, Koeppen, Wenders, and Gert Hofmann, among others, and is the translator of the last four Joseph Roth titles to appear in English: *Right and Left, The*

Legend of the Holy Drinker, The Tale of the 1002nd Night (for which he won the PEN/Book-of-the-Month Club Prize), and *Rebellion*, and hopes to bring out collections of Roth's journalism and shorter fiction.